CHRISTMAS

The Annual of Christmas Literature and Art

CHRISTMAS

CHRISTMAS

The Annual of Christmas Literature and Art

VOLUME SIXTY-ONE

AUGSBURG FORTRESS, MINNEAPOLIS

In this volume

Christmas is for the children, some would say. And, perhaps, it *is* true that children are most captivated by the twinkling lights, the promise of presents, the aroma of cookies baking, and the stories of the season. Yet, inside of all of us there seems to hide a child who doesn't want to grow up, who hopes each year to experience anew the wonder and excitement of Christmases past. That is the magic of Christmas, the innocent, wide-eyed amazement and breathless anticipation that makes the season like no other.

Volume 61 of CHRISTMAS celebrates the spirit of the child in this collection of holiday reading. Three articles explore activities various children (and adults) enjoy at Christmastime. "Christmas Across the Footlights" features the holiday productions of The Children's Theatre Company in Minneapolis, the second largest children's theater in the world. "Whistles from the Past" traces the history of toy and model train collecting, and "Visions of Sugarplums" offers readers a baker's dozen of traditional cookie recipes from around the world to try.

Young and old alike will enjoy the fanciful tale, "The Song of the Owl," which explains why the owl flies around asking, "Who-o-o?" And the humorous poem, "A Cow's-Eye View of Christmas," about the manger birth is sure to become an annual favorite. For the very young person, "A Christmas Alphabet" uses playful illustration to tell the story of Jesus' birth.

We are sure you will enjoy the beautiful artwork and photography that accompany each page, starting with Frank Wesley's colorful and unusual portrayal of "The Christmas Story." Also showcased in these pages is one of Grandma Moses's childlike paintings, *White Christmas*, along with a brief description of this delightful woman and her work.

Many other treasures fill the pages of this year's volume of CHRISTMAS. May your celebration of the Savior's birth be all the richer because of what you discover here.

—THE EDITORS

Table of Contents

Editorial Staff: Gloria E. Bengtson, Jennifer Huber, Sandra Gangelhoff.

Advisory Committee: Carol Erdahl, Carol Evans-Smith, M. Alexandra George, Mary Lohre, Cynthia Nelson.

Design: Koechel Peterson & Associates, Inc.

The Christmas Story

According to
St. Luke & St. Matthew

And it came to pass in those days that a decree went out from Caesar Augustus that all the world should be registered. This census first took place while Quirinius was governing Syria. So all went to be registered, everyone to his own city.

And Joseph also went up from Galilee, out of the city of Nazareth, into Judea, to the city of David, which is called Bethlehem, because he was of the house and lineage of David, to be registered with Mary, his betrothed wife, who was with child.

So it was, that while they were there, the days were completed for her to be delivered. And she brought forth her first-born Son, and wrapped him in swaddling cloths, and laid him in a manger, because there was no room for them in the inn.

The Annunciation to Mary
(page 5)

shows Mary seated in front of a mud and thatch house, surprised in the midst of her task of winnowing grain. The purple color of her sari emphasizes her distinction as stated by the heavenly messenger: "Rejoice, highly favored one, the Lord is with you; blessed are you among women!" (Luke 1:28) Purple is the mixture of blue and red— blue symbolizing eternity and red symbolizing the earth, creation, and joy. The angel is holding a lotus, which represents holiness and purity. The banana and mango trees stand for growth and fruitfulness.

The Nativity
(page 7)

shows the holy family in a mud hut, such as those where cattle or buffalo are kept, but never sheep or donkeys. Joseph is dressed in ordinary Indian style. The color red represents happiness. Orange as the mixture of red and yellow symbolizes a man who has lived an honest and pious life.

Now there were in the same country shepherds living out in the fields, keeping watch over their flock by night. And behold, an angel of the Lord stood before them, and the glory of the Lord shone around them, and they were greatly afraid.

Then the angel said to them, "Do not be afraid, for behold, I bring you good tidings of great joy which will be to all people. For there is born to you this day in the city of David a Savior, who is Christ the Lord. And this will be the sign to you: You will find a babe wrapped in swaddling cloths, lying in a manger."

And suddenly there was with the angel a multitude of the heavenly host praising God and saying:

"Glory to God in the highest,
And on earth peace, good will toward men!"

So it was, when the angels had gone away from them into heaven, that the shepherds said to one another, "Let us now go to Bethlehem and see this thing that has come to pass, which the Lord has made known to us." And they came with haste and found Mary and Joseph, and the babe lying in a manger.

Now when they had seen him, they made widely known the saying which was told them concerning this child. And all those who heard it marveled at those things which were told them by the shepherds. But Mary kept all these things and pondered them in her heart. Then the shepherds returned, glorifying and praising God for all the things that they had heard and seen, as it was told them.

The Announcement to the Shepherds
(page 9)

contains no specific Indian symbolism, but shows the heavens opened to reveal the angels' singing.

NOW AFTER JESUS WAS BORN IN BETHLEHEM OF JUDEA in the days of Herod the king, behold, wise men from the East came to Jerusalem, saying, "Where is he who has been born King of the Jews? For we have seen his star in the East and have come to worship him."

When Herod the king heard these things, he was troubled, and all Jerusalem with him. And when he had gathered all the chief priests and scribes of the people together, he inquired of them where the Christ was to be born.

So they said to him, "In Bethlehem of Judea, for thus it is written by the prophet:

'But you, Bethlehem, in the land of Judah,

Are not the least among the rulers of Judah;

For out of you shall come a Ruler

Who will shepherd my people Israel.' "

Then Herod, when he had secretly called the wise men, determined from them what time the star appeared. And he sent them to Bethlehem and said, "Go and search diligently for the young child, and when you have found him, bring back word to me, that I may come and worship him also."

When they heard the king, they departed; and behold, the star which they had seen in the East went before them, till it came and stood over where the young child was. When they saw the star, they rejoiced with exceedingly great joy.

And when they had come into the house, they saw the young child with Mary his mother, and fell down and worshiped him. And when they had opened their treasures, they presented gifts to him: gold, frankincense, and myrrh.

Then, being divinely warned in a dream that they should not return to Herod, they departed for their own country another way.

The Visit of the Magi
(page 11)

portrays three Eastern wise men. The first, an Indian, is depicted as a pious scholar leading an ascetic life. Behind him stands an Iranian nobleman, followed by a Chinese scholar.

Now when they had departed, behold, an angel of the Lord appeared to Joseph in a dream, saying, "Arise, take the young child and his mother, flee to Egypt, and stay there until I bring you word; for Herod will seek the young child to destroy him."

When he arose, he took the young child and his mother by night and departed for Egypt, and was there until the death of Herod, that it might be fulfilled which was spoken by the Lord through the prophet, saying, "Out of Egypt I called my Son."

But when Herod was dead, behold, an angel of the Lord appeared in a dream to Joseph in Egypt, saying, "Arise, take the young child and his mother, and go to the land of Israel, for those who sought the young child's life are dead."

Then he arose, took the young child and his mother, and came into the land of Israel.

THE ARTIST

Frank Wesley was born in north India into a family of mixed Hindu and Moslem descent. Recognized early on for his talent, he attended the Government Art College in Lucknow on scholarship and completed his five-year course with distinction. As a fourth-generation Christian, Wesley is deeply interested in using Indian symbolism to present the life of Christ. Thousands of reprints of his works have been distributed throughout India. The artist now lives and paints in Australia.

The Flight to Egypt
(page 13)

captures Joseph, Mary, and the infant Jesus fleeing Bethlehem on foot during the night. Commenting on the refugee status of the holy family, the artist writes: "Coming from crowded Asia, I still find it hard to take that they (their own people) didn't find room for one pregnant traveler. There is always room for one more in our buses, trains, village houses, cities, and roadside shelters!"

Christmas Across the Footlights

ANN WOODBECK

(above) *Young Beatrix Potter, as played by Angela Ness, smiles as she thinks of her imaginary friends in* Beatrix Potter's Christmas.

A beautiful young girl is poised at the window. Her face is filled with wonder as she stares past her reflection into the wintry night. It has been a splendid Christmas—her first in 12 years.

She smiles, thinking of the new friends that have opened her heart to the spirit of the season: the Squirrel Nutkins, Mr. and Mrs. Puddle-Duck, the hedgehog Mrs. Tiggy-Winkle, and the Flopsy Bunnies. Hearing her parents in the hallway, she hurries away from the window. She wishes she could find a way to share her secret joy with them. But today, young Beatrix Potter is content to keep her secret with the spellbound audience of the largest children's theater in America—The Children's Theatre Company of Minneapolis.

In the lobby after the performance, wide-eyed children gather around the huge Christmas tree decorated with garlands of nuts and berries. Larger-than-life rabbits and cats in gingham dresses greet the young visitors, posing patiently for photographs that will capture the magic of the evening. A worried five-year-old boy pushes his way past the forest creatures to grab the hand of Beatrix Potter. "Are you okay?" he implores. For 13-year-old Angela Ness, the talented lead actress in *Beatrix Potter's Christmas*, it is a touching and familiar moment. The cruelty of Beatrix' parents has struck a chord in this child and his concern was genuine, honest in the way that only children can be.

Respect for the integrity and honesty of children has guided The Children's Theatre Company from its beginnings. In 1965, artist and visionary John Clark Donohue invited a handful of talented, energetic people to join a repertory company that would introduce young people to the best in live theater and children's literature. In its first official home at the Minneapolis Institute of Arts, company members did it all: wrote the plays, directed, performed, built the sets, sold the tickets, and did the bookkeeping. Today, the company resides in a remarkable theater complex that houses a full-time professional staff of

14

82 artists, technicians, and administrators, a state-of-the-art scene shop, wardrobe shop, dance studio, studio theater, and a vast 750-seat main stage auditorium. More than 100 original scripts based on classic and contemporary children's stories have been lovingly adapted for The Children's Theatre Company (CTC) stage, complemented by the orchestration of 108 original musical scores.

Each year, CTC performs for over 300,000 children and their families during its regular season and reaches more than 100,000 people through its national touring program. Determined to enhance the theater's international reputation, the company initiated an historic exchange with the world's largest theater for children, The Central Children's Theatre of Moscow, in 1989. The year 1991 holds the promise of an exchange with The Children's Art Theatre in China.

Donohue's successor, Artistic Director Jon Cranney, presides over the nine member, full-time acting company. Actor Gerald Drake is one of two founding members who have remained with the company throughout its 26-year history. The greatest challenge in working with young actors, according to Drake, is helping them learn to open their hearts to the audience. It is not always easy, even for stage veterans, to share a part of oneself with an audience, but the support of fellow actors eases the way. The sense of unity that bound the company together in its early days is still vital to the company today.

David Ira Goldstein, Associate Director of Seattle's A Contemporary Theatre, directed CTC's 1989 production of *Cinderella*. The success of CTC, he believes, is based on their belief that working for

and with children is the most important work in theater. Goldstein acquired his love of theater while attending CTC shows in its early days. Donahue's legacy demands that CTC's work must be better because it is for children; it cannot be second-rate, think-

The Little Match Girl *portrays the harsh realities of poverty, but ends on a hopeful note when she is reunited with her beloved grandmother.*

ing that children won't know the difference.

In addition to providing a learning lab for young professionals coming out of college and professional programs, Jon Cranney believes that the mission of CTC is to create a new generation of theatergoers. Often, parents will stop Cranney after a performance to tell him that they started coming to the theater as chil-

dren and now delight in bringing their children to the shows. Providing a link between generations, CTC has become an important tradition for families throughout the upper Midwest. Many families travel from as far away as North Dakota, South Dakota, Iowa, and Wisconsin to attend the theater's productions, especially during the holidays. It is a festive time in the city, an opportunity to shop for Christmas gifts, marvel at gaily decorated display windows, and to celebrate the season with friends and relatives. An evening at CTC is often the highlight of their holiday vacation.

The criteria for selecting a

play for the Christmas productions are simple. First and foremost, the play must capture the spirit of the season. Christmas celebrates the family and holiday audiences are filled with families of every make and description. For many families, this may be the only theater performance that they will attend all year. It is the sharing of the story within the family, according to Goldstein, that makes it so special. The story is usually classic in the sense that it is familiar to even the youngest members of the audience, allowing them to participate in the performance. And finally, the play must be spectacular. Music and dance are important elements of each Christmas production. Sets and costumes are lavish, dramatic, and elaborate. For the company, Christmas productions are very demanding physically. The performance schedule is equally rigorous with two shows each day; six days a week.

THE CAST

Even by CTC standards, the casts for Christmas productions are large. Over 100 aspiring young performers arrive each year to audition for roles in the chorus. According to Production Stage Manager Donna Bachman, veteran young CTC actors don't have any special advantage over newcomers. In fact, according to Director David Ira Goldstein, casting the chorus can be the time to take a chance on a youngster who has auditioned several times and needs a smaller role to break into the theater scene. Often, the impression a young actor makes may be cumulative: after a number of auditions, Artistic Director Jon Cranney may point out a persistent and promising candidate to the casting director.

Part of the selection process involves the director's instinct. He or she looks for the person who can make things seem familial, enjoying the interaction with others on the stage. Blendability, according to Donna Bachman, is another important characteristic. A pleasing combination of size, hair, and skin colors creates a colorful picture on the stage. Everyone brings a little bit of their own life to the stage in even the smallest part and that is what gives the production a lively, vibrant feeling. Most of all, Bachman observes, a performer must be able to transcend the barrier of space between the actors on the stage and the audience. They must be able to get the love out to the audience. Every member of the cast, from the chorus to the lead, has a great sense of giving a gift to the audience, especially at Christmastime.

TIME-HONORED CLASSICS

The Children's Theatre Company's signature piece, *Cinderella*, is unquestionably the theater's most popular Christmas production. Renowned child psychologist Bruno Bettelheim calls *Cinderella* the best-known and best-liked fairy tale of all time. He traces its origins to ninth-century China, where tiny foot size was a mark of extraordinary beauty and virtue. It is, in the French version on which the play is based, a story of sibling rivalry to which nearly every child can relate.

CTC presents the play in the style of the traditional festival pantomime plays (or panto) that have been popular in English theater for the past two centuries. Panto evolved from the traditions of Italy's *commedia dell'arte*, combining

a traditional fairy tale with outrageous humor, high energy, glamour, romance, and a number of running inside jokes that involve the audience. The CTC staging is presented with the distinctive Victorian flavor of the nineteenth century.

In the engaging panto style, the audience is prodded and cajoled into active participation with the cast. Gerald Drake plays the wicked stepmother with spirited, campy zeal, dressed in high Victorian fashion, complete with powdered wig. Children delight in the permission to talk back to the character, championing the cause of the poor, downtrodden heroine. In her 26-year history with CTC, Wendy Lehr has performed the role of Pearl, the despicable stepsister, in all eight of CTC's stagings of *Cinderella*. She is a character that audiences love to hate. In 1990, Lehr directed this production for the first time. Each production is unique, as each performer and director is encouraged to make their distinctive mark on the production. During the show, the wicked stepmother fires a pistol into the air to demand the ensemble's attention and a rubber chicken falls from the rafters. When David Ira Goldstein directed the play, he replaced the chicken with a life-size foam-rubber cow that plummets to the stage floor. The ensuing hilarity nearly brings the house down. These are the elements that make *Cinderella* the favorite of the cast, as well as the audience.

The Prince's Ball never fails to enchant the young romantics in the audience. Dressed in their own holiday finery, the audience thrills to the sight of splendid gowns in pale ivory and the formal powdered wigs that adorn the dancers at the ball. Elaborately carved and

gilded columns and staircases create an elegance beyond our childhood dreams. Cinderella's Fairy Godmother dances her spell in the snow-covered fairy-tale garden and transforms Cinderella's rags into a gorgeous gown of the purest

Cinderella, CTC's most popular Christmas production, engages the audience with its outrageous humor, high energy, glamour, and romance.

white satin and lace. Actress Charity Jones recalls being mesmerized by the Cinderella story as a young girl. Years later, playing the heroine of the play, she wondered if she would be able to convey the innocent sincerity that draws a young audience into the story. Afterward, in the lobby, her youthful fans reassured

her that she had done her job convincingly. "I have you on videotape," one little girl told her, "only you have on a blue dress." That childlike acceptance and willingness to believe both humbles and motivates the company. Jones

finds the ending of the play its highpoint. When timid Cinderella is denied the chance to try on the glass slipper, the audience screams for her to be recognized. Forced to submit to the audience's demand, the wicked stepmother stands over Cinderella and snorts, "It will never fit." And in every performance, one little voice from the balcony yells out, "Oh, yes it will!"

For Gerald Drake, the real beauty of the Cinderella story lies in the forgiveness that transforms not only Cinderella, but her cruel family as well. The theater receives let-

ters from patrons criticizing the cruelty of the stepmother, though the CTC version isn't nearly as harsh as the original tale. Drake believes that for the tale to work, there must be some pain to overcome. It is like watching a tightrope walker, he observes, who pulls us in by faltering and nearly falling. The excitement would be lost if the acrobat could just saunter across the wire.

Hans Christian Andersen's *Little Match Girl* is perhaps the most controversial of the theater's Christmas selections. It is a hauntingly beautiful tale of an innocent child who dreams of escaping from her harsh life with an abusive father. In the dark, cold streets, she sells matches to passersby to earn the money on which she can barely survive. Ignored by holiday revelers, she is taunted by the delicious odors of the Christmas feasts that linger in every doorway. Fearing her father's retribution, the frail child curls up in a protected corner and lights a match to chase away the biting cold. For a brief moment,

she imagines sitting near a warm, welcoming stove. As the match flame fades, she finds herself back in her snowy corner. Striking a new match, she thrills to the sight of a richly set table, covered with a feast fit for a king. This, too, vanishes and she is moved to light another flame. This vision is one of an incredible toy shop, in which every toy she has ever longed for appears. When the flame disappears with her vision, she sees a falling star. Her beloved grandmother, now deceased, had told her that "when a star falls, a soul is going up to God." With her next strike, her grandmother appears in the circle of flame. Knowing that this vision will fade as the others have, the Little Match Girl ignites a handful of matches. She is gathered into the loving arms of her departed grandmother and together "they soar in a halo of light and joy, far above the earth, where there was no more cold, no hunger, and no pain—for they were with God."[1]

The story touches a painful reality of life in poverty that exists even today. For some, the hope that shines through the story's end is not enough. Jon Cranney theorizes that parents critical of this choice for a Christmas play want to choose another time to expose their children to the harsher realities of life. Many of its supporters believe that the loving atmosphere of the Christmas season makes it the perfect time to recognize that such difficulties do exist.

Somewhere between the gaiety of *Cinderella* and the sobering aspects of *Little Match Girl* fits the story of *Beatrix Potter's Christmas*. In this production based on the tales of Beatrix Potter, audiences come to love a lonely

young girl who creates her own Christmas celebration with the forest creatures from her imagination. This piece is a testimonial to the brilliant design work of CTC's costume shop. Human-size animals in remarkable recreations of Potter's squirrels, mice, cats, rabbits, and even a benevolent hedgehog create a fantasy world that delights young and old. Its conclusion transforms the lonely girl into a hopeful, happy child who learns, on this Christmas Day, that she can create joy and wonder from the goodness of her own heart.

CONTEMPORARY WORKS

CTC balances its schedule of time-honored classics with work by contemporary writers as well. It has earned an international reputation for its ability to recreate the storybook page on the stage. The rich palette of Tomie de Paola's *Strega Nona* comes alive on the CTC stage in *Merry Christmas, Strega Nona*. Fancifully rounded characters dominate the stage in this beloved Italian tale of a benevolent grandma witch. When her assistant, the endearing bungler Big Anthony, is dispatched to shop for Christmas gifts, he drops the packages down a steep hill. Trying to retrieve them, he rolls himself into a huge snowball. In the village, Strega Nona awaits the groceries that will create the magnificent Christmas feast. Magically, she manages to create her memorable meal in spite of Big Anthony's misadventures.

The spirit of the season is enhanced each year by artful-

[1] Andersen, Hans Christian, *Little Match Girl*, New York, G. P. Putnam's Sons, 1987, p. 28.

ly crafted olios, a collection of musical pieces borrowed from the English tradition. Between scenes of the performance, small groups from the chorus regale the audience with traditional and innovative inter-

production of *Peter Pan* from the company's repertoire delighted 45,000 people on CTC's main stage and 40,000 more succumbed to the charm of *Cinderella* at St. Paul's O'Shaughnessy Auditorium.

and throughout the school year. Educators prepare students for the play with the help of a specially prepared theater guide. With this tool, students learn more about each production, its history

and warmth of the holiday, The Children's Theatre Company focuses its outreach efforts in January and February, sending costumed characters to cheer the young people who face illness and

Fanciful rounded characters dominate the stage in Merry Christmas, Strega Nona, *an Italian tale about a benevolent grandma witch and her bungling assistant, Big Anthony. An example of CTC's renowned staging, this set recreates the rich palette of Tomie de Paola's storybook version of the tale.*

pretations of the season's carols. In the lobby, visitors join the company for a magical, musical celebration.

THE COMMUNITY

The Christmas shows at CTC sell out well in advance of the first performance of the season. In an effort to remain accessible to every family in the upper Midwest region, the theater added a second holiday production to its 1990-91 season. The first Christmas

One gauge of community support lies in the growth of season ticket holders from 7500 in 1984 to nearly 26,000 in 1991. Sponsorship by locally based corporations has enabled the theater to continue its traditions of excellence.

In addition to its performing traditions, CTC reaches out to the theatergoing community in several ways. Busloads of school children fill the theater for special daytime performances during the holiday season

and psychology. Classes are encouraged to take advantage of related literature and activities available within the community. Before and after the play, young people are encouraged to explore their own interpretation and feelings about the theater experience.

Moved by the spirit of Christmas, many community organizations make time to visit children in hospitals and group homes in the cities. Hoping to prolong the joy

separation from family.

For several years, the theater has invited patrons to share their celebration with less fortunate families through donations to Santa Anonymous. The generous response has grown with each year.

In celebration of God's greatest gift to the world, Christmas inspires people everywhere to share the blessings and gifts that enrich our lives. Across the footlights at The Children's Theatre Company, the tradition lives on. ✿

The Woodcarver's Gift

BARBARA J. HAMPTON

ZELE WAS DREAMING OF THE DOLL when her older brother shook her awake. It was a big doll with yellow curls and a frilly pink dress. Every day for a week now she had gone in to look at it on the counter of the store near where her mother made market.

"Do you want to buy this doll? No? Maybe you will get it for Christmas! It is coming soon," the storekeeper had finally said to her yesterday.

Zele had turned away sadly. Her large family did not celebrate Christmas as a few people in their village did, and even if they had there wasn't enough money for such a beautiful doll. Nevertheless, she fell asleep dreaming of the doll's yellow curls and big blue eyes, so different from her own stiff black plaits and solemn brown eyes. But now the doll faded from her mind with her brother's rough words.

"Get up, Last Girl. Grandfather is ill. We must bring him to the hospital. Our mother says you must carry his clothes and his rice."

Grandfather ill? Zele's stomach felt hollow. Grandfather, who always had a kind word for her, the youngest of the family's many children. Grandfather, who helped her with her many chores so she could join the others already at play. Grandfather, who told her tales when the kerosene lamps were lit but it was too early to sleep, tales he had heard as a boy. Not Grandfather.

The girl got up and slipped on her shirt and wrapped her lappa skirt around her. She obedient-ly gathered up the supplies and went in search of a taxi to take them to the hospital. It was past many villages, too far for Grandfather to walk.

The air was still cool, though light was beginning to streak the sky as she hurried down the path. The roosters scattered away from her, but a kid goat tagged along behind. Zele rubbed his head for a minute and felt him nuzzle her. Then she quickened her steps. She knew the taxi driver would be angry because she would awaken him. She would do it, though, because Grandfather needed her.

When they arrived at the hospital, long lines had already formed. They found their places at the end of one of them and waited. People moved forward slowly, staring ahead or scolding a child or chewing on peanuts or a banana. A few boys laughed as they played keep-away with rocks until their

mothers shooed them away from the waiting people. Now Zele's fear and hunger gnawed more persistently, but no one spoke to her or gave her food. She sat and waited.

Finally their turn came. Her mother spoke quickly and sharply to the man at the first table and Zele's empty stomach knotted as she heard her mother's voice: "Hot ... dry ... cough." These words echoed and frightened her. Then Grandfather was taken away and she was left alone.

"What is wrong, my little one?" Zele looked up. Where were the kind words coming from? An old man, maybe as old as Grandfather, sat by a table. On the table were many clean, empty bottles, which he handed to people who came past him. She stared at him in spite of herself, for he had no legs. His smile was soft as he repeated, "What is wrong?"

"My grandfather. . . ." Zele stumbled then and couldn't continue. Could this man know how she felt? Suddenly she caught sight of her mother and, smiling shyly at the old man, ran to meet her.

"Grandfather must stay here and so must you," her mother told Zele. "You will cook his rice every day and sleep on the mat under his bed and do what the nurses tell you to do. I am going now."

Zele was numb with the news but she obeyed her mother. She went into the hospital and searched among the beds until she found her grandfather's. She put down her small bundle and the bag of rice and sat down to wait again. The nurses were busy, for every bed was full. Some people were even lying on the floor. At last a young woman in a blue-striped dress stopped at the bed. She showed her how to make Grandfather comfortable and where to get water for him to drink.

Early the next morning she went into the hospital courtyard to prepare their rice. A woman from the village next to hers let Zele pound her rice in the big mortar after she herself was finished using it. Then Zele washed and cleaned the rice and set it over the fire to cook. The other people were not unkind to Zele, but they paid little attention to her. She was just a quiet dark shadow as they called to each other and talked of the sick family members they were there to care for. Zele did not tell any of them about her grandfather.

Zele cooked the rice as best she could, the way she had learned at home in the village, but Grandfather did not eat much of it. Mostly he slept, though he tried to smile at her when she smoothed his sheets. "My little Zele," he would murmur.

"How is your grandfather?" asked the man who had no legs. Zele had left Grandfather sleeping and had come back to him through the

long lines of people. He had remembered! Zele's heart skipped a beat and she blurted out, "He's ill. He won't eat much. I'm afraid." But then she stopped.

"You love him, my little one," the old man said, briefly laying his hand on her black plaits. "Stay here by me for a while." Soon Zele was no longer staring at his legs but at his hands, for when he was not handing bottles to people, he was carving. The dark

> The dark wood gleamed in his hands as he shaped figures. In his fingers they seemed almost alive.

wood gleamed in his hands as he shaped figures—small antelopes, monkeys and goats, tiny women and babies. In his fingers they seemed almost alive.

Grandfather slept so much and there was so little she could do for him that Zele went back to the carver the next morning, too. After a couple of days he asked, "Would you try to find some dark wood, like this, in the forest over there? Not large pieces, but see, they should look like this." He showed her the piece of wood he was holding, a red-brown color, straight and round.

Zele gladly ran off. Near the hospital she passed a group of children. Some were hammering boards together, some were singing, and others were just playing.

A girl caught sight of Zele and called her to join them. But Zele didn't stop until she was behind the building, where she lingered to watch two young goats who were playing hide and seek. When she laughed aloud at them the spotted one trotted after her into the bush.

The sun warmed Zele. She suddenly felt happy as she searched through the tangle of vines and dead leaves for the wood. She began to hum the song she had heard the children singing.

She brought three pieces of wood back to the carver. She wasn't sure they were good enough because they were not smooth, but he said to her, "You have an eye for wood." He turned them over and over in his hands. "These will make beautiful figures."

His words reminded Zele of the beautiful doll. She wondered to herself if he would understand her wish to have that doll. Grandfather would, she knew, but talking with him only made him too tired. She had to tell someone! Shyly still, she described the doll and her pink dress to the old carver. "The storekeeper said the doll is for Christmas," Zele finished.

"You do love beauty, my child," the carver said, more to himself than to her, and again he gently laid his hand on her head. He sighed as he removed it. "Then tonight come out and see something beautiful. It is Christmas Eve when the children of the hospital chapel will act out an old story. It is a true story, the most beautiful one ever known."

"I will come," Zele promised, and went back to Grandfather's hospital bed.

But Grandfather did not eat anything that afternoon. He did not even smile or open his eyes. Zele sat by his bedside, wondering if she should leave him and becoming more lonely and

afraid. She knew, though, that she would feel better if she could be with her friend, the old carver. And so, at last, when it became dark, she slipped from the mat on the floor and crept out into the courtyard. People were gathering and soon they were singing and clapping, gourds shaking and drums beating in accompaniment.

Zele looked around. She recognized the women who cooked each morning in the courtyard, but she did not see any of the children. She guessed that they would be in the play. Finally she saw the carver. Zele sat down next to him, quietly, so as not to disturb his pleasure in the music. But he looked down at her and smiled, and suddenly she felt as though she too could share in the joy of the evening.

A hush settled over the crowd. Their faces gleamed in the light of the lanterns. Zele caught her breath as a small girl dressed in a long white lappa came forward. No longer was she the girl who had called out to her this morning. She was the angel who told Mary that she would have a baby.

In the soft light, the Christmas story unfolded before Zele. Joseph and Mary made their slow journey to Bethlehem; they were turned away at the inn. The baby Jesus was born and laid carefully in the manger. Angels sang to the shepherds who left their sheep and came to worship the baby. Three kings, dressed in many-colored gowns, brought beautiful gifts to him.

Reluctantly Zele turned her eyes away when the last king had disappeared. She wished that the story could last forever, but people were laughing and greeting each other and were

turning away to serve the evening's feast.

"What did you think?" the old carver asked.

"It was so beautiful," she answered simply.

"Not only beautiful, but true. That baby grew up and made the way back to our Father God for us. He will be your friend, too, Zele."

Her grandfather was dying, Zele knew that. But she had friends, the friend Jesus and her friend the carver. She tiptoed back to Grandfather, lay down, and went to sleep. This night she slept deeply, not dreaming of the pink doll but of angels and shepherds and a baby.

When she awoke early on Christmas morning a nurse told her that Grandfather had died. Feeling very empty and alone, Zele wrapped up her small bundle and went to say good-bye to the carver. She must return to her village and tell her family so that someone could come for Grandfather's body.

"Merry Christmas, small Zele. Your Grandfather?" The carver's voice was a question and Zele cried as she told him. He gath-

ered her in his arms and let her cry. Then he set her down and gave her a small package. "Take this home now, Zele, and remember your old friend. Maybe it will help you remember the shepherds who worshiped the best friend of all."

Zele turned to leave. When she could no longer see the hospital she stopped. Her fingers fumbled as she tore open the plain paper wrapping. There in her hands lay two wooden figures. A girl and a goat. The old carver had made them just for her. They were hers to play with, hers to remember the shepherds by, and hers to love for the beauty of the rich brown wood. Zele wrapped up her Christmas gift and walked on home.

A COW'S-EYE VIEW

DAWN FINLAY

I was a cow in the
 year number one,
and the first
 Christmas Day had
 only begun;
the rooster crowed
 and up came the sun.
I went to the door, as
 I did every day,
to stand in line for my
 breakfast hay
and listen to what the
 donkey might say.

The donkey was there
 and a pigeon or two,
so I greeted them all
 with a bright morning
 "moo."
The donkey brayed,
 and the pigeons said,
 "Coo!"
We waited and waited
 for ever-so-long,
and the sweet smell
 of hay was
 ever-so-strong,
and someone was singing
 a lullaby song!

The stable looked
different (but there
was no danger)—
a beautiful lady sat
by the manger.
Well, that was strange,
but something was
stranger!
The sweetest,
tiny baby lay
sound asleep in my
breakfast hay.
That's when I bowed
my head to pray.

Then as I knelt on
the floor's hard sod,
I somehow knew—
though this was
odd—
I knew that the babe
was the Son
of God!
"God," I prayed (but
it came out "moo"),
"O God, what
wonderful things
you do!"
The donkey brayed,
but the pigeons
said, "Coo!"

Visions of Sugarplums

SUZANNE P. CAMPBELL

No one knows when the first cookies were made but they were probably similar to hard cakes or biscuits. Indeed the French word for cookie, *gateau sec*, means "dry or hard cake." Our American word *cookie* probably comes from the Dutch *koekje*, or "little cake." Cookies are fun to make and even more fun to eat. They are part of the Christmas tradition in countries all over the world.

Ingredients, however, vary from nation to nation. Africans often bake with cornmeal instead of flour; in India flour is replaced by ground chickpeas; and Scandinavians leaven the dough with hartshorn instead of baking powder or baking soda. Indeed, cookies are such an important part of the holidays in Norway that the first great thaw after Christmas is called the "cookie thaw," as though the heat from all the ovens was responsible for melting the snow! Following are a baker's dozen of cookie recipes that might be made this Christmas by families all over the globe. Why not try some and enjoy an international holiday!

HOLLAND

In Holland the festival of St. Nicholas is celebrated on the evening of December 5, called *Sinterklaas avond* (the eve of St. Nicholas Day). The saint, it is said, always rides a white horse. Children fill their shoes with straw and carrots for the horse and leave them by the fireplace. They hope that St. Nicholas will exchange their offerings for small presents or treats. The most popular Christmas cookies are called *speculaas*, or "mirrors," because the molds used for the recipe make cookies that exactly reflect the molds themselves.

DUTCH SPECULAAS
2 cups all-purpose flour
2 tsp. ground cinnamon
1/2 tsp. baking powder
1/2 tsp. ground nutmeg
1 tsp. ground cloves
1/8 tsp. salt
1/4 cup ground blanched almonds
1 cup firmly packed brown sugar
3/4 cup firm butter or margarine cut into pieces
2 tbsp. milk

1. In a large bowl, stir together flour, cinnamon, baking powder, nutmeg, cloves, and salt.

2. Blend in almonds and sugar until well combined.

3. With a pastry blender or 2 knives, cut in butter until mixture resembles cornmeal; stir in milk.

4. Work dough with your hands until you can form it into a smooth ball.

5. For molded cookies: Press dough firmly and evenly into a floured wooden speculaas mold; invert onto an ungreased baking sheet and release cookie by tapping the back of mold (ease cookies out with the point of a knife, if necessary). Space cookies about 1 inch apart.

For rolled cookies: On a lightly floured board, roll out dough to a thickness of about 1/4 inch. Cut out with 2- to 3-inch cookie cutters. Transfer to ungreased cookie sheets, spacing cookies about 1 inch apart.

6. Bake in 300°F oven for 20 to 30 minutes for large cookies and 20 to 25 minutes for small cookies or until lightly browned. Let cool briefly on baking sheets; transfer to racks and let cool completely. Store in airtight containers.

Makes about 4 dozen or 4 large speculaas.

GREECE

Greek children enjoy butter cookies all year long. At Christmastime the cookies are covered with a mantle of snowy powdered sugar and decorated with a whole clove to symbolize the spices brought by the Magi to the baby Jesus. (The cloves are removed before the cookies are eaten.)

GREEK BUTTER COOKIES (KOURABIETHES)
(Recipe by Lynne Villios)
2 1/2 cups all-purpose flour
1 tsp. baking powder
1/4 tsp. salt
1 cup butter, softened
1/2 cup sugar
1 egg
1/2 tsp. vanilla extract
1/2 tsp. almond extract
powdered sugar for sprinkling
whole cloves, if desired

1. Preheat oven to 350°F.

2. In a small bowl, combine flour, baking powder, and salt.

3. In a large bowl, beat together butter, sugar, and egg until light and fluffy.

4. Add flour mixture to butter mixture and mix until blended.

5. Add vanilla and almond extracts and mix well.

6. With your hands, form dough, about 1/2 tablespoon at a time, into balls, crescents, or S-shapes; press in 1 whole clove (if desired).

7. Place cookies 2 inches apart on a cookie sheet. Put on middle oven rack and bake 15 to 18 minutes or until lightly brown around the edges.

8. Remove from cookie sheet and cool on wire rack for 5 minutes.

9. Sprinkle cookies with powdered sugar.

Makes about 3 dozen.

MEXICO

Mexican street vendors sell these holiday treats in the town plazas on Christmas Eve. Instead of on a paper napkin, *buñuelos* are served on cracked or chipped pottery plates. It is the custom to eat the treat and then break the dish by throwing it on the ground. Many believe this tradition is connected with ancient Indian ceremonies in which the broken pottery symbolized the ending of the old year.

MEXICAN BUNUELOS
(Recipe by Rosa Coronado)
4 cups all-purpose flour
2 tbsp. sugar
1 tbsp. baking powder
2 eggs
2 tbsp. milk
1/4 cup vegetable oil
1 cup warm water
1 cup vegetable oil
(for frying)
1/2 cup sugar
3 tbsp. cinnamon

1. Thoroughly mix flour, sugar, and baking powder in a large bowl.

2. In another bowl, beat together eggs and milk. Then add to dry ingredients. Stir in 1/4 cup oil and mix well.

3. Add warm water and mix well until dough can be handled easily. (If dough is too dry, add a few more teaspoons of warm water, one at a time.)

4. Place dough on a lightly floured board and knead until smooth.

5. Divide dough into 20 to 24 pieces and shape each into a ball. Flatten balls on the board with the palm of your hand. Cover with cloth for 20 minutes.

6. On a lightly floured board, roll out each flattened ball with a rolling pin into a large round shape about 6 or 7 inches in diameter. Let stand 5 minutes.

7. Heat 1 cup oil in an electric frying pan set at 360°F. (If you don't have an electric frying pan, use a fat thermometer to check the temperature of oil heated in a regular frying pan.) Just before frying, stretch each buñuelo a little more by hand.

8. Fry each buñuelo until underside is golden brown (about 3 minutes). Turn and fry other side until crisp. Remove and drain on paper towel.

9. In a small bowl, combine sugar and cinnamon. Sprinkle hot buñuelos with cinnamon and sugar mixture.

Makes 20 to 24.

POLAND

Christmas supper is served in Poland as soon as the first star appears in the sky on Christmas Eve. A place is set for any stranger who may appear and there is an extra chair ready to welcome the Christ child. The children especially look forward to dessert when they will eat *Mazurkas*. This traditional Polish cookie is often made with two or three layers. In this version the bottom layer is a cookie crust and the topping a simple coating of jam.

POLISH MAZURKAS (MAZUREK)
Basic Dough:
2 cups shelled almonds, blanched and ground
1 cup unsalted butter plus extra to grease pan
(you can use half margarine)
1 cup granulated sugar
4 eggs
2 tbsp. milk
1/4 tsp. salt
2 cups all-purpose flour

1. Preheat oven to 350°F. Grease jellyroll pan. Grind almonds in food processor, blender, or chopper. Set aside.

2. In mixing bowl, beat together butter and sugar until creamy. Add eggs one at a time, then milk, and beat well. Add flour, a little at a time, beating slowly until combined. Stir in salt and ground nuts.

3. With back of large spoon, spread batter evenly over greased pan. Bake at 350°F for 20 minutes or until golden brown. Remove from oven. While still warm, spoon jam over top of cookies (see below).

Jam Topping:
1 cup jam, such as apricot, raspberry, or strawberry
powdered sugar

Cool about 5 minutes, then cut into bars. Lift onto wire rack to cool. When cold, lightly sprinkle with powdered sugar. You should be able to see some of the jam color beneath the sugar.

Makes 70 bars, 2 inches x 1 inch.

GERMANY

In Germany Christmas is called *Weihnachten*, or "Watch Night." It is the Germans who brought us many familiar Christmas customs, among them decorated Christmas trees. The Germans often hang edible decorations such as these *Zimtsterne* or "cinnamon stars" on their trees. *Zimtsterne* are also enjoyed in Switzerland.

GERMAN-SWISS ZIMTSTERNE
3 tbsp. butter or margarine
1 1/2 cups sugar
2 whole eggs
1 egg, separated
1 tsp. lemon juice
2 1/3 cups all-purpose flour
2 1/2 tsp. baking powder
1 1/4 tsp. cinnamon
1/4 tsp. salt
1/4 tsp. nutmeg
1/2 cup finely chopped walnuts

1. Heat oven to 375°F.

2. Mix butter, sugar, 2 whole eggs, 1 egg yolk, and lemon juice until fluffy.

3. Measure flour. Stir dry ingredients together; blend into sugar mixture. Stir in nuts.

4. Divide dough into thirds. Roll out dough on a lightly floured board to 1/16-inch thickness.

5. Cut with 3-inch star cutter.

6. Brush tops of cookies with beaten egg white.

7. Bake on lightly greased baking sheet 6 to 8 minutes.

Makes 6 dozen.

SCOTLAND

In Scotland New Year's Eve is called *Hogmanay*. Whoever first enters the door after the clock rings in the New Year is called the "first footer." This person, by tradition, brings either good or bad luck to the household for the rest of the year. The best "first footer" is a handsome stranger. Sometimes a member of the family goes out and comes back in as the "first footer," bringing traditional gifts that symbolize warmth and prosperity. These gifts include a piece of coal, some bread, salt, money, and Hogmanay shortbread. The shortbread must be made with the finest unsalted butter in order to have the proper rich, buttery taste.

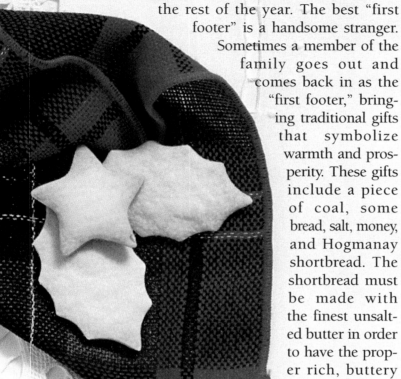

SCOTCH HOGMANAY SHORTBREAD
3/4 cup unsalted butter or margarine
1/4 cup sugar
2 cups all-purpose flour

1. Mix butter and sugar thoroughly.

2. Measure flour and work in with hands.

3. Heat oven to 350°F.

4. Roll out dough to 1/3- to 1/2-inch thickness. Cut into fancy shapes (small leaves, ovals, squares, etc.). Flute edges if desired by pinching between fingers as for pie crust.

5. Place on ungreased baking sheet. Bake 15 to 20 minutes. (The tops do not brown during baking, nor do the shapes of the cookies change.)

Makes about 2 dozen.

BRAZIL

Since 90 percent of the people in Brazil are Roman Catholic, most families attend a special Christmas midnight mass called *Misa de Gallo*. Worshipers bring gifts of food for the needy, wrapped in white paper, and lay them in a simple manger in the front of the church. Christmas cookies in Brazil often include the famous Brazil nuts. The nut trees grow wild only in this country's tropical rain forests. Each towering tree can produce a thousand pounds of the nuts in one year. The cookie that follows has a candy-like texture.

BRAZILIAN LACE WAFERS
1/4 cup soft butter
1 1/2 cups firmly packed light brown sugar
2 tbsp. water
1 cup all-purpose flour
1 tsp. ground cinnamon
1 1/2 cups finely chopped Brazil nuts

1. In a bowl, cream butter and blend in brown sugar and water. Stir in flour, cinnamon, and nuts. Shape mixture into 60 balls. Place 6 on greased baking sheet, 2 inches apart.

2. Preheat oven to 325°F. Bake for 15 to 20 minutes or until cookies are spread thin and are browned on the edges. Let cool 30 seconds, then remove from baking sheets with a pancake turner and cool on racks. Store in an airtight container in a cool, dry place.

Makes 60.

AFRICA

Throughout West Africa the most popular sweet is a cookie made with peanut butter or peanuts, which are grown in the area. For only a penny you can buy one from street vendors in most cities and towns. This cookie is nutritious as well as tasty and, best of all, requires no cooking. Peanuts can be used instead of peanut butter, in which case they are pounded together with sugar using a wooden pestle.

AFRICAN KANYA
(KAHN-yah)
or PEANUT BARS
1/2 cup smooth peanut butter
1/2 cup superfine sugar
2/3 cup Cream of Rice (uncooked)

1. Combine peanut butter and sugar in a bowl and blend well using a wooden spoon.

2. Add Cream of Rice, a little at a time, and continue pounding each time.

3. Turn the mixture into a 8-inch x 4-inch loaf pan and press it down evenly with your fingers. Cover the pan with waxed paper or plastic wrap and chill 2 or 3 hours until firm.

4. Remove from pan and cut into small bars with a table knife.

Makes 20.

CHINA

Traditionally, the Chinese did not eat sweets but embraced the custom with enthusiasm when it was introduced by Westerners. Now the almond cookie is available in almost all Chinese bakeries. Because the Chinese do not raise many cattle, the principal meat eaten is pork, and dairy products are rarely available. Lard is rendered from pork and used for shortening in place of the butter used in other nations. You can make this recipe with butter or vegetable shortening, but it won't taste quite the same.

HANG GEEN BENG (Hahng geen bee-EHNG)
or CHINESE ALMOND COOKIES
1 cup all-purpose flour
1/2 cup lard (shortening or 1/2 butter-1/2 margarine
    may be substituted)
1/2 tsp. salt
1/4 cup plus 2 tbsp. sugar
1/2 tsp. almond or vanilla extract
1 egg yolk
1 tbsp. water
1/4 cup blanched almonds

1. Combine flour and shortening.

2. Work salt, sugar, and flavoring in with hands.

3. Shape into long roll 1 inch in diameter, wrap in waxed paper, and chill for about 1 hour.

AFTER 1 HOUR:

4. Heat oven to 400°F.

5. Cut dough in 1/4-inch slices. Place about 1 inch apart on lightly greased baking sheet.

6. Brush each cookie with a mixture of egg yolk and water. Press 1/2 blanched almond in top of each cookie.

7. Bake 8 to 10 minutes or until light golden brown. Allow cookies to cool slightly before removing from baking sheet so they won't crumble.

Makes about 2 dozen.

HUNGARY

Sometime after the first snowfall in Hungary, the red hoods of Father Winter begin appearing in shop windows and the fir trees arrive from the mountains to fill homes with Christmas beauty. Then it's time to do the holiday baking. In Hungarian, *Estike*, the name of a favorite cookie, means "evening fairies." Because the cookies must sit out overnight to become crisp, people believed that fairies came to taste these delicious confections and keep watch over them. The recipe contains no baking powder because the lemon juice gives the treats a lighter texture.

HUNGARIAN ESTIKE (esh-TEE-keh)
or EVENING FAIRIES
2/3 cup all-purpose flour
2 eggs
1/2 cup sugar
1 tbsp. lemon juice
1 tsp. vanilla extract
1/8 tsp. salt
1/4 tsp. anise seed

1. Line baking sheets with parchment paper.

2. Beat eggs in mixing bowl until thick and pale in color, approximately 5 minutes.

3. Gradually add sugar and continue beating for a few minutes.

4. Add lemon juice, vanilla, and salt and beat 5 more minutes.

5. Gradually add flour and mix.

6. Drop by teaspoonfuls on parchment-lined baking sheets. Drop 2 or 3 anise seeds on top of each cookie. Put the baking sheets in a safe place where they can stay uncovered overnight.

THE NEXT DAY:

7. Preheat oven to 300°F. Bake cookies 12 to 15 minutes until they are dry but not brown. Remove from oven and baking sheets; cool on wire rack.

Makes about 5 dozen.

SCANDINAVIA

Gingersnaps are a popular year-round snack in Scandinavian homes. Yet, for many families it just wouldn't be Christmas without the aroma of these spicy treats wafting from the oven. The cookies have as many names as there are countries in the Northland. In Sweden they are known as *Pepparkakor*, in Denmark as *Brune kager*, in Finland as *Piparkakut*, and in Norway as *Pepperkaker*.

GINGERSNAPS
2/3 cup dark corn syrup, slightly warm
1/2 cup softened butter
2/3 cup sour cream
1 1/2 cups sugar
1 1/2 tsp. ginger
1 tsp. cloves
2 tsp. cinnamon
3 tsp. baking powder,
    dissolved in 2 tbsp.
    water
3 1/2 cups flour

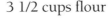

1. Mix all ingredients except flour in bowl.

2. Gradually add 3 1/2 cups flour.

3. Cover and refrigerate overnight.

THE NEXT DAY:

4. Preheat oven to 400°F.

5. Generously grease baking sheets.

6. On well-floured board or pastry cloth, roll dough to 1/4-inch thickness with well-floured rolling pin.

7. Cut out cookies with round or fancy cutters dipped in flour.

8. Place on prepared baking sheets.

9. Bake 8 to 10 minutes.

10. Cool on baking sheets before removing to rack.

Makes about 20 dozen.

RUSSIA

When Christmas guests arrive in a Russian home, the table kettle or *samovar* is heated to boil water for tea to accompany these special mint cookies. Sometimes the cookies are piled into little paper baskets as Christmas tree decorations. The following recipe was a favorite of Alexandra Tolstoy, daughter of Leo Tolstoy whose writings include such famous books as *War and Peace*. She remembered the cookies from her Russian childhood when wood-burning stoves were used for all cooking and baking.

RUSSIAN MIATNIYE PRIANIKI
(mee-Yaht-nee-yeh pree-AH-nee-kee)
or MINT COOKIES
1 cup milk
1/2 tsp. hartshorn (ammonium carbonate)*
1 cup sugar
1 tbsp. corn oil
8 drops peppermint oil (can be purchased
from the drugstore)
3 1/4 cups all-purpose flour
pinch of salt

*An inexpensive white powder that acts like baking powder to make cookies and cakes rise in baking. You can buy it at the drugstore.

1. Preheat oven to 350°F. Grease baking sheets.

2. Heat milk in a small saucepan just to boiling point when little bubbles appear on the surface.

3. Pour milk into a mixing bowl, add the hartshorn, and mix well.

4. Add sugar, corn oil, and peppermint oil. Mix well.

5. Combine flour and salt and add to the milk mixture. Stir until smooth.

6. With floured hands, roll small pieces of dough to make small balls 1 inch in diameter.

7. Arrange on baking sheets.

8. Bake 10 to 12 minutes. Do not allow to brown. Remove from oven and baking sheets. Place on a wire rack to cool.

Makes about 3 1/2 dozen.

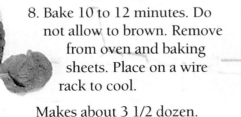

ICELAND

Cardamom is a spice frequently used for Christmas baking in Iceland but is less well known in America. It was first brought to Iceland by the Vikings who discovered it on their sailing expeditions through the Middle Eastern spice trading centers centuries ago. This cookie is a traditional favorite, especially at Christmastime.

ICELANDIC HALFMANAR (Half-ma-nahr)
or HALF-MOONS
2 1/2 cups all-purpose flour
2/3 cup sugar
1/2 tsp. baking powder
1 tsp. ground cardamom
1/2 tsp. hartshorn (ammonium carbonate)*
1 1/3 cups butter or margarine
1 egg
1 10-oz. jar prune butter (lekvar)

*An inexpensive white powder that acts like baking powder to make cookies and cakes rise in baking. You can buy it at the drugstore.

1. Sift together flour, sugar, baking powder, cardamom, and hartshorn.

2. Cut butter into small pieces and add to flour mixture.

3. Work ingredients together with fingers until well blended.

4. In a small bowl beat the egg lightly with an egg beater or wire whisk and add to dough. Mix well with spoon.

5. Chill the bowl of dough in the refrigerator for one hour.

AFTER ONE HOUR:

6. Preheat oven to 350°F. Grease baking sheets.

7. Generously sprinkle flour on a pastry board and place dough on board.

8. Roll with floured rolling pin to about 1/4-inch thickness.

9. Cut out circles with a round cookie cutter or drinking glass.

10. Arrange on baking sheets.

11. Put 1/2 tsp. prune butter on each cookie. Fold cookies over to cover filling and form half-moon shapes.

12. Carefully press edges of cookie with fork dipped in flour.

13. Bake 10 to 12 minutes. Remove from oven and baking sheets. Place on wire rack to cool.

Makes 5 to 6 dozen.

White Christmas

Grandma Moses (1860-1961)

ARTICLE BY PHILLIP GUGEL — *White Christmas (on page 33)* presents Grandma Moses at her best. Looking at this bird's-eye view of a winter landscape, we can even imagine that it is Grandma herself who stands with arms widespread in a warm welcome at her home's front door, greeting the visitors who draw near in their sleighs. Blanketed by newly fallen snow, Grandma Moses' landscape has a freshness about it typical of her other snowscapes. (In some of her earlier snow scenes, she even sprinkled mica particles on them so they would sparkle.)

The variety of white tonalities she used are evocative of winter in the Hoosick Valley of upstate New York, which nourished her imagination. *White Christmas* delights us with its colorful portrayal of activities.

As Grandma Moses herself noted, she liked to use bright colors and show plenty of human activity in her pictures (of which there are over 1500). Both of these traits stand out in *White Christmas*. The painting shows brightly clad folks arriving by sleigh at the quaint farmhouse. Children are playing at classic winter activities: building a snowman, skating, and sliding. A mood of cheeriness and festivity prevails. It recalls a time when Christmas celebrations were more humanly and less materially centered.

Using oil and tempera paints, Grandma Moses painted *White Christmas* in 1954 on a masonite board. As she explained briefly in a section of her autobiography, she developed her own method of starting a picture. First, she would find a frame she liked and then she would saw a board to fit the frame's dimensions. Next she applied a coat of linseed oil to seal the board's surface and three coats of flat white paint as a primer. Finally, she was ready to begin painting. She preferred to paint on a hard wood or masonite surface because it would last much longer than canvas. It seems Grandma wanted to impart some of her durability and longevity to her pictures as well!

We can appreciate *White Christmas* for its joyous mood and genuine nostalgia, which Grandma Moses so skillfully captured, even though her capabilities as a self-taught painter in depicting figures, perspective, and scale were somewhat limited.

A number of notable persons, including actor Lillian Gish and composer Cole Porter, enjoyed and collected Grandma Moses' paintings. *White Christmas*, appropriately enough,

Grandma Moses at her painting table. Photo by Ifor Thomas. Copyright © 1987, Grandma Moses Properties Co., New York.

was acquired by Irving Berlin, who composed that classic American song, "White Christmas," made famous by Bing Crosby.

Perhaps one reason why people from many walks of life find the pictures she painted appealing is that Grandma Moses herself was such an engaging and interesting person. Anyone who reads her autobiography, *My Life's History*, will find she expresses herself in it with the same directness and simplicity found in her paintings.

Born September 7, 1860, Anna Robertson showed an interest in painting in her earlier years and occasionally dabbled in it. Yet, she was a widow and a grandmother nearing 80 years old before a physical condition led her to start painting regularly. Arthritis in her hands forced her to give up needlework; so her sister Celestia, who also painted, encouraged her to take up painting. She did so and enjoyed it, but did not take it seriously at first. It was simply a hobby, until several fortuitous events created a demand for her pictures and placed Grandma Moses (as she was affectionately called) on the road to recognition.

Someone suggested that she display her work in the Hoosick Falls drugstore. A collector happened to see the paintings and encouraged Otto Kallir, the owner of an art gallery in New York City, to exhibit and sell them. Both were taken by the naive character of her works and by the fact that she painted only what she knew, a key to her art.

Despite her limited formal education, Grandma Moses was an intelligent and perceptive woman who learned much from life experiences. Married to Thomas Salmon Moses in 1887, Grandma shared in the work on farms they owned in Virginia and New York. She highly valued her husband, with whom she raised five children. Nevertheless, she had her share of tragedies—four other children were stillborn and one lived only six weeks. Thomas died in 1927. Yet Grandma seemed to accept all things in her life with a certain grace, a sign of her strong faith.

Her personality made a strong impression on all who encountered her. She was charming, cheerful, generous, good-natured, kindly, lively, modest, and self-effacing. Yet, she had definite ideas about things and did not hesitate to go her own way, even in her painting.

At her age, Grandma Moses did not coddle any pretensions about her

art. She painted to please herself. In fact, the pleasure that others found in viewing her pictures may have surprised her.

A sense of humor allowed her to make light of her accomplishments and not to become easily upset by others' remarks about her art. She was not impressed with the awards, exhibits, honorary degrees, interviews, and speaking invitations that recognition brought, though she did enjoy the personal contact she had at these events. Her enjoyment of people and activity is evidenced in the important place they have in her paintings.

On her ninety-third birthday Grandma Moses offered this recipe for health and long life: ". . . good eatin's and good keepin's." When asked of what she was most proud she replied, "I've helped some people."

She was a remarkable woman who enriched other peoples' lives through her humane spirit and deep faith. Concluding a television interview with her on June 29, 1955, Edward R. Murrow asserted that when Grandma Moses died, she would leave more for us to cherish than most people. Posterity has certainly proven him right.

MARY

Based on Isaiah 7:14; Luke 1:1-56; Matthew 1:18-25

MARGARET A. GRAHAM

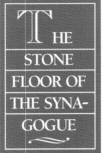

THE STONE FLOOR OF THE SYNAGOGUE was cold beneath her feet but Mary scarcely noticed, straining as she was to hear the man who was praying. She knew by heart all the prayers of the *Shemoneh 'Esreh*—three in praise of God, 13 petitions, and three thanksgivings. Today, only the first and last three prayers would be recited, with a single prayer substituted for the 13 omitted. The voice droned on, barely audible in the far reaches of the women's section. Bored, the women chatted with one another and gave no heed to what was being spoken.

Mary tried hard to keep her mind from wandering, although it was difficult with Joseph sitting on the other side in clear view. She dare not cast a sidelong glance at him lest the women chide her. Nathan, Joseph's friend, was faithful in going back and forth between them, and plied Mary with credits in Joseph's favor. "Not everyone can trace his ancestry," Nathan told her. "But Joseph's ancestry is carefully preserved because he is of the house of David."

What mattered most to Mary was that Joseph was a fair man, and a hard-working, skilled carpenter. He would not undertake marriage if he was not able to support a wife and family.

Mary remembered the evening a year before, when Joseph's father and Nathan had come to speak with her father—first with a promise of marriage, later to make the betrothal covenant. There were gifts of garments and a garnet necklace for her. Both families gathered in the courtyard of her father's home with witnesses to attest the covenant. Red of face, Joseph placed a gold ring on her finger saying, "See by this ring you

are set apart for me, according to the law of Moses and of Israel."

With appropriate modesty her eyes met his, and in that one swift glance the earnestness in his young face made her feel glad inside.

Even so Mary, young as she was, had misgivings that she may not measure up as a wife among the more mature women of Nazareth. "They bake, they sew," she fretted, "they take care of children, work in the vineyards, the olive groves—" She sighed. "Perhaps he'll change his mind."

"Don't worry," Nathan told her, "only a breach of the betrothal vows can break the covenant. A breach of the vows would be considered adultery, which never could happen with you. But even if it did, Mary, the betrothal could be dissolved only by divorce. Joseph loves you, silly girl. And, unless I am deceived, you love him." He cocked his eye at her questioningly but, seeing no response, continued. "Think of it this way, Mary—in a few months you'll be a married woman with your very own home with no one to look after but Joseph and his old father, Jacob."

The prospect filled her with

anticipation and her imagination ran away with her. When the prayer ended Mary caught herself daydreaming and, feeling sorry, turned her attention back to the service.

The ruler of the synagogue asked a young man to read from Moses. He was the leather-worker's son, the one who wished to become a scribe. Blond and fair skinned, he mounted the raised platform nervously. With a grave expression on his face he unrolled the scroll for the reading of the day; but when he could not find the place amused women tittered behind the lattice that shielded them from view. The ruler came to the boy's aid. Flustered, his prayer shawl slipping down the back of his head, the youth began. In an unsteady voice he read from Deuteronomy in Hebrew and, verse by verse, translated it into Aramaic.

Mary listened carefully, recording the words in memory for she could scarcely read. Unlike Jewish boys, who attended synagogue school, she knew only what her mother had taught her at home. All schooling was by rote, and Mary's mind was trained to memorize quickly and easily. Turning the phrases over and over in her head, as with her sister Salome, they became the warp and woof of her life.

Even so, she envied the elders sitting on the front row who not only could read but spent most of their time studying the Torah. She wondered if other women yearned as she did for more knowledge of the Scriptures.

No more than 50 people attended Sabbath services, for Nazareth was a small village and not all its villagers were Jewish. Of those 50, 17 were women. Three Greeks attended irregularly and considered themselves to be God-fearers but not proselytes, for they were not circumcised.

Mary tried hard to keep her mind from wandering, although it was difficult with Joseph sitting on the other side in clear view.

After the Deuteronomy passage there followed the reading from the prophets. Clumsily the young man struggled with the scroll until he found Daniel. As he read, Mary knew the sermon would raise lively debate among the men.

When the reading of Scripture was finished, an elder, chosen by the ruler, took the seat before the chest containing the scrolls and delivered the sermon. With keen logic he sought to convince the congregation that Daniel's 70 weeks were about to run their course. The other elders interrupted noisily, registering their disagreements, while one old man slept, his chin on his chest and snoring loudly. Farmers and the like, too intimidated by the leaders to raise their voices, listened eagerly, wanting most of all to believe the Messiah would soon come.

The sermon ended but the heated discussion was only momentarily suspended. In the absence of a priest, a prayer substituted for the benediction followed by the congregation's "Amen." Then the debate resumed noisier than before.

Mary did not linger to talk with the women nor to wait for Salome, who would stay and chat, but hurried outside to be well on her way home before the worshipers disbanded. Neither did she want Nathan to come chasing after her. She had given him a message for Joseph, which he would deliver after the service, and it would be unseemly to appear to be waiting for an answer so soon.

A short distance from the synagogue were the precipitous cliffs, some of them as high as 50 feet, and walking along the edge Mary enjoyed the view in the early April night. Moonlight streaming down over Mount Tabor cast a luminous mantle of pearl, softening the harsh ridges, molding the shapes of stones.

Winding between Mount Tabor and the hills of

Nazareth was the ancient Great Road West, or the Way of the Sea, a caravan route from the distant East to the distant West. Past the Hill of Precipitation, the steep road from Jerusalem climbed up to enter Nazareth, and to the northeast a road dropped down to the Sea of Galilee by way of Cana. All her life Mary had observed the heavily laden travelers, wondering what exotic wares they carried, and watched Roman soldiers in their scarlet capes going to and from their military posts.

As she took the road descending into town, Mary could see most of the village spread out below. Nazareth, its white limestone houses nestled in a basin surrounded by a low-lying escarpment, was sometimes ridiculed for its bad manners and morals. Its reputation aside, Nazareth in moonlight was as fair a place as one could seek. Mary could think of no other place as home. To her the houses were beautifully situated among fig trees, olive groves, and the graceful, slender cypress, unequaled even in Capernaum. Down about the village well were gardens, surrounded by prickly-pear hedges, where vegetation thrived.

The dusty road was rutted from the wheels of wagons, and animal droppings made her cautious as she walked. In her heart she felt a certain joy that gave her the urge to skip along the road but, it being the Sabbath, she restrained herself. Passing between two houses, one with a dovecote on the roof, she listened for the contented cooing sounds of birds roosting there. But as she drew alongside, something startled the doves; all at once they flut-

tered from their nests and, flocking into the air, flew up and away.

Surprised and somewhat puzzled, Mary paused at the gate of the second house. Suddenly, a man appeared out of nowhere.

"Greetings," he said, "you who are highly favored! The Lord is with you."

Startled, Mary did not know what to think. His words so troubled her she could not speak.

~

H*er heart thumping in her chest, Mary realized he was not an ordinary man. He's an angel of God!*

~

"Do not be afraid, Mary, you have found favor with God." He moved a step closer, and laid his hand on the gate.

Her heart thumping in her chest, Mary realized he was not an ordinary man. *He's an angel of God!*

"You will be with child and give birth to a son …"

The words baffled her. *With child? Give birth?*

"You are to give him the name Jesus. He will be great and will be called the Son of the Most High."

Whatever does he mean? she wondered, her heart pounding.

"The Lord will give him the throne of his father David, and he will reign over the house of Jacob forever; his kingdom will never end."

Her lips dry, her heart palpitating wildly, Mary's mind was racing. *I'm not married. How*—Totally confused, she blurted out, "How will this be since I am a virgin?"

The angel glanced up at the flock of doves returning, then replied, "The Holy Spirit will come upon you, and the power of the Most High will overshadow you."

Stunned, she was barely aware of the doves swirling overhead, their wings beating, seeking out their nests.

"So the holy one to be born will be called the Son of God," he told her, his voice strong and reassuring.

Astonished as she was, a certain joy began to take hold of her. Then the angel added this: "Even Elizabeth your relative is going to have a child in her old age, and she who was said to be barren is in her sixth month." He paused, looking down at her kindly. "For nothing is impossible with God."

Mary's hands were cold, her body trembling. Returning the man's kindly gaze she said as simply as she knew how, "I am the Lord's servant. May it be to me as you have said."

Acknowledging her submissiveness with a nod of his head, and while she was still looking at him, the angel disappeared.

Mary felt profoundly shaken and it was some time before, unconsciously, she began to move along. Walking ever so slowly, her thoughts raced.

No one must know of this, she resolved. *Not even Salome. Certainly no one would believe— He will be called the Son of God!...What would father think? What if—I dare not imagine what the neighbors in Nazareth will say if they get wind of this.*

Hearing voices in the distance, Mary quickened her step lest the returning worshipers overtake her.

That night, lying on the pallet beside her sister, Mary waited until steady breathing assured her that Salome was sleeping. Then, sitting up, she let go the worries that would disturb her and, reviewing what the angel had told her, became excited. "Call him Jesus, Son of the Most High—" Such words are beyond me! *"Give him the throne of his father David—"* This child, this baby will sit on David's throne? Fulfill the covenant...bring to pass God's promise to David! Oh, can it be that I... that this child to be born to me is to be a king...a king over a kingdom that will never end!

In her excitement she had forgotten the news about Elizabeth, and

remembering that she, too, was being favored, Mary was beside herself with joy. Elizabeth's miracle called to mind Hannah who had also been barren, although not as old as Elizabeth, and the great joy Hannah expressed when God gave her a son. Mary had found it easy to learn Hannah's hymn of praise and, being somewhat poetically gifted herself, Mary began making up in her mind her own hymn of joy using scriptural phrases and words of her own.

~

Astonished that Elizabeth already knew of her condition, Mary was eager to hear more.

~

Not once did she close her eyes. All night long her mind went back and forth from the ecstatic to the sublime as she pondered what the message meant and considered what practical action to take.

As day began to dawn Mary had made up her mind; but because it was the Sabbath she waited until the first day of the week to carry out her plan. The angel's mention of Elizabeth seemed to be a directive, the proper course to pursue. Packing a few garments, some food, and water, she prepared for the journey to visit Elizabeth. Without telling her father or Salome the reason, she left on horseback, traveling in the company of a family going to Emmaus.

Mary was anxious to reach Elizabeth, for if anyone would understand her situation Elizabeth would. For a woman who was past the age of childbearing, one who had always been sterile, to have a child was a miracle. The angel's words declared it: *"For nothing is impossible with God."*

Elizabeth's case reminded Mary of barren Sarah, Abraham's wife, who was more than 90 years old when she bore the son from whom all Jews on the face of the earth descended. *Surely he is the God of the impossible, Mary thought, ... and there were also the barren wives of Isaac and Jacob. Elizabeth's miracle is not the first of its kind.*

As the horse beneath her kept to his steady gait, Mary considered the reproach Elizabeth had suffered in not being able to bear a son—so shameful was her plight, rabbis had told her husband a separation was their religious duty. Mary thought about how often they must have cried out to God, weeping. How many sleepless nights did they walk the floor before they gave up hope thinking their prayer was denied.

Now, Mary realized, *all that heartache is past—Elizabeth will cradle a son in her arms!* Joy welled up in Mary's soul and words of praise flowed easily. The lyrical rhythm lent itself to a melody, and Mary hummed the song as she rode on ahead of the others.

Camping that night, Mary sat up long after the family had bedded down in a cave. Watching the embers of the campfire dying, the Holy Spirit seemed to consume her, giving her such joy she could not contain herself. Looking up at the stars she whispered her praise to the Almighty God, her cheeks wet with tears of gratitude.

On the third day the traveling companions reached Emmaus. From there it was only a short ride to the village where Elizabeth lived.

Zechariah was standing in front of the house when Mary rode up the dusty street, and he greeted her with a wave of his hand. Mary dismounted and spoke to him, but he didn't reply. She handed him the reins, puzzled by his silence.

As she entered the house Mary called out, "Peace!" Elizabeth, turning around, exclaimed, "Blessed are you among women, and blessed is the child you will bear!" Her wrinkled face was radiant!

The women reached out their arms to each other. As they were embracing Elizabeth drew back and asked, "But why am I so favored, that the mother of my Lord should come to me?" Clutching Mary's hand, she led her to the table. "As soon as the sound of your greeting reached my ears, the baby in my womb leaped for joy."

Astonished that Elizabeth already knew of her condition, Mary was eager to hear more. The spirit of prophecy was upon the older woman in a way Mary had never known before.

Elizabeth's eyes brimmed with tears. "Blessed is she who has believed that what the Lord has said to her will be accomplished!"

In the silence that followed, Mary heard nothing but the beating of her own heart. The awesome fullness of God exhilarated her.

Mary bowed her head. From somewhere deep inside her, the Holy Spirit was prompting words of praise—scripture phrases and her own words knitting together in Hebrew rhythms such as she had heard all her life. In a voice so low she scarcely heard it herself, the words poured forth:

My soul praises the Lord,
and my spirit rejoices in
God my Savior,
for he has been mindful
of the humble state of his
servant.

Elizabeth reached for her hand and held it in both her own. Hannah's words of praise came to mind, and for one brief moment Mary felt joined to all women blessed of God in special ways:

From now on all generations will
call me blessed,

for the Mighty One has done
great things for me—
holy is his name.

In the silence that followed, she heard nothing but the beating of her own heart. The awesome fullness of God exhilarated her, and the words flowed freely:

His mercy extends to those
who fear him,
from generation to
generation.
He has performed mighty deeds
with his arm;
he has scattered those who
are proud in their inmost
thoughts.

Mary closed her eyes. Not a Babylonian or Persian prince had stood long against the Lord, nor would the Romans prevail. The King was coming! Little Israel, heir of the promises made to Abraham, would be exalted, favored by God:

He has brought down rulers from
their thrones
but has lifted up the humble.
He has filled the hungry with
good things
but has sent the rich away
empty.
He has helped his servant Israel,
remembering to be merciful
to Abraham and his descendants
forever,
even as he said to our fathers.

When the hymn ended, the two women sat quietly worshiping God, overwhelmed by the mystery of what was taking place.

After taking care of the horse, Zechariah came inside and joined Mary and Elizabeth at the table. As he was unable to speak, Elizabeth spoke for him, explaining to Mary about Gabriel's visit to Zechariah.

For the next three months Mary remained with Elizabeth and Zechariah, helping with the chores, praying, talking. But when it was time for Elizabeth's son to be born Mary packed her things and bid them farewell. It was time to tell Joseph. ❖

SONG
OF
THE
OWL

MARGARET L. TENPAS

Long, long ago, before the first Christmas, the owl did not act the way he does now. In fact, he slept at night, just like the other birds. During the day he flew through the trees, just like the robins and bluejays and eagles. He hunted blackberries and cherries, and sang a happy, trilling song.

But one evening, when all the birds had returned to their nests, the sky seemed different. The black night did not close around them with its usual silence. Instead, high in the heavens there shone a star, bright and dazzling, more bright and dazzling than any star the birds had ever seen.

The sparrows chirped and the bluejays chattered, questioning what the star could mean. But the owl, who had been extra busy that day trying to impress his sweetheart by bringing her berries and grasshoppers, could think only of sleep. So he tucked his head beneath his wing, closed his eyes, and drifted off into warm, pleasant dreams.

Then, from far away, he heard a voice calling, calling. At first the owl pretended not to hear, but finally, as the voice came closer, he lifted his head and looked down the path that wound through the forest. In the bright light from the star, the owl saw a sight that seemed most strange.

There, seated on camels, appeared three richly dressed men. Each wore a crown that twinkled in the light. Their capes were edged in fur and, with the movement of their hands, light glittered from the rings on their fingers.

The men on the camels stopped beneath the trees, and the tall one in the center spoke. "Waken, waken, sleeping birds. Come join us in our journey. You will not be sorry. For we go to Bethlehem to greet our newborn King. The star will lead us. Come, come now, for the child awaits us."

From all the trees came flutterings and murmurings, and then a great rush of wings as the cardinals and robins, the wrens and the sparrows, the bluejays and the plovers formed in line behind the men on their camels.

But the owl did not move. His nest felt warm and soft. The air outside was cold and Bethlehem was far away. Grumbling at the noise, he muttered, "Who? Who? Who bids me follow?"

He heard no reply. And so, lazy and sleepy, he settled back on his warm nest and slept.

When morning came, the owl found the forest strangely silent, for all the other birds had followed the three kings. Only the owl had remained behind. But he sang as he searched for food, thinking how easy it was with none of the others around. He didn't have to outwit the hawk or fly faster than the eagle. In no time at all he felt very, very full.

That night, just as he had settled back on his warm, smooth nest, he heard the rushing of wings, and the trees trembled. Voices of many birds beat about his ears.

"So beautiful, so blessed, so wonderful," the voices sang.

At these words the owl became curious and roused himself.

"Who? Who? Who are you chattering about?" he asked.

And then the others told him about the baby Jesus, so calm and serene, lying in the manger. And the birds spoke of the angel chorus chanting, "Glory to God in the highest and on earth peace, goodwill to all."

And as the angels sang, the animals knelt in the straw while the three kings gave their gifts of gold, frankincense, and myrrh. And all the while the great star shone over the stable where the King of kings lay, the tiny baby Jesus.

Now, at last, the owl understood "who." And he was ashamed. Why had he stayed behind? Now he would never see the wonderful child.

From that moment on the owl changed his habits. No longer does the owl fly about during the daylight hours, singing a happy song. Instead he waits until night to begin his singing. For he wants to keep reminding the world of the wonderful birth, to make everyone remember who it was that came into the world. So, over and over, he repeats the question, "W-h-o-o? W-h-o-o? W-h-o-o?" ❖

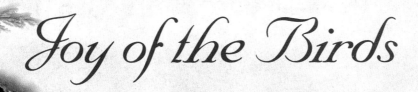

Joy of the Birds

BETTY HARMON

*"Some say that ever 'gainst that season comes
Wherein our Savior's birth is celebrated,
The bird of dawning singeth all night long
So hallow'd and so gracious is the time."*

SHAKESPEARE, *HAMLET*, ACT I, SCENE I

Birds and Christmas go together! Christmas is a time of beauty. The bright plumage of the cardinal or the bluejay seen against the snow-laden bough of an evergreen compares in beauty with the most gaily decorated Christmas tree. Christmas is a time of good cheer. The cheerful chirping of sparrows, chickadees, and finches can lift our spirits on the grayest, most dreary days of winter. Christmas is a time when God's grace is seen anew. Birds lend their "grace notes" to this gracious time.

Birds are special creatures in God's creation. In teaching his disciples about God's love and care, Jesus admonished them to "Look at the birds of the air" (Matthew 6:26). In our love for the Christmas season, let us "look at the birds of the air," the birds in some of the carols of Christmas.

Christmas carols from many lands include a wide variety of birds: nightingales, doves, finches, cuckoos, sparrows, and larks. Birds, because they abound in field and forest, were among the first to learn of the birth of the newborn King proclaimed by the angelic host and the brilliant star. The French carol "Whence Comes This Rush of Wings" from Bas-Quercy paints the scene as many birds respond to the glad news of Christ's birth in Bethlehem:

*Whence comes this rush of wings afar,
Following straight the Noel star?
Birds from the woods in wondrous flight,
Bethlehem seek this holy night.*

The mention of Philomel is of particular interest in this lovely carol. According to Greek mythology, Philomela was a Greek goddess who was turned into a nightingale. In many poems and literary works, the nightingale is called Philomel, a melodic name for this bird of the thrush family that sings so sweetly at night.

The nightingale is also referred to in the traditional Catalonian "Carol of the Birds." Stanza two says: "The nightingale is first to bring his song of cheer," perhaps because he sings before the dawn breaks. "Sweet Nightingale, Awake," a traditional German carol, calls upon this sweet songster to "trill the news most joyfully . . . sing to hail the newborn King."

Although its song is not as sweet as the nightingale's, the cock (or rooster) may also be numbered among the birds who sing in the darkness. The fifteenth-century English nativity carol, "Chanticleer," tells us how the cock expresses his joy at the coming of God's only Son:

All this night shrill Chanticleer,
Day's proclaiming trumpeter,
Claps his wings and loudly cries,
Mortals, mortals, wake and rise!
See a wonder
Heaven is under;
From the earth is risen a Sun
Shines all night, though day be done.

Later in the seventeenth century, the cock appears in a curious carol based on a legend of "King Herod and the Cock." The Magi, according to this legend, tell Herod of "a princely babe born that night" that no king can destroy. King Herod points to a roasted cock in a dish upon his table and declares that if their story is true the dead cock will crow three times. Whereupon the carol concludes:

The cock soon thrusted and
*   feathered well*
By the work of God's own hand,
And he did crow full fences* three,
In the dish where he did stand.

Birds, being first upon the Bethlehem scene, use their varied voices to sing the praises of God's gift. One of the happiest groups of praising birds is in the Czech carol, "The Birds." The translation given here was taken down from a Czech peasant girl the Christmas of 1921 at Policka in   the hills between Bohemia   and Moravia by a Miss Jakubickuva.
         One can almost hear the cuckoo's song, the pigeon's "vrercroo," and the dove's gentle "tsucroo." As is the case of most folk songs passed from generation to generation by oral tradition, the words are simple and lively!

*times

The birds of Christmas are examples of true giving. They not only give their songs of praise, they also give the very best they have. In the twelfth-century English carol, "The Friendly Beasts," each animal offers a distinctively individual gift to Jesus. The donkey gives its strength by carrying Mary safely to Bethlehem. The cow gives its manger for Christ's first little bed. The sheep brings wool to warm the new babe. Then the dove speaks:

"I" said the dove from the rafters high,
"I cooed him to sleep so he would not cry,
We cooed him to sleep, my mate and I."
"I" said the dove from the rafters high.

Think of the tenderness of the dove, gently lullabying both Jesus and his young mother as they lay in unfamiliar surroundings. Then add to this the touching gift of the bird in the Slovakian carol, "*Pan Jezisku*" ("Small Lord Jesus"). She brings a part of her own small body:

The bird in her nest
Gave down from her breast
To soften the rest
Of the small Lord Jesus.

As we draw near the manger, the whole sky fills with the rush of many wings and the happy caroling of many voices as winged creatures of every land tell of their ineffable joy at the birth of Jesus Christ. God the Creator has entered creation as a human, the Man for all seasons:

Now every bird that flies in air,
Sing raven, lark, and dove:
The night has brooded on her lair
And fledged the bird of love.
Sing sweet as the flute,
Sing clear as the horn,
Sing joy of the birds,
Come Christmas the morn.

ELEANOR FARJEON

Whence Comes this Rush of Wings Afar

Traditional French
tr. anon

Traditional Bas-Quercy Carol

1. Whence comes this rush of wings a - far
2. "Tell us, ye birds, why come ye here,
3. Hark how the green - finch bears his part,
4. An - gels and shep - herds, birds of the sky,

fol - low-ing straight the no - el star?
In - to this sta - ble, poor and drear?"
Phil - o - mel, too, with ten - der heart,
Come where the Son of God doth lie;

Birds from the woods in won - drous flight,
"Hast" - ning we seek the new - born King,
Chants from her leaf - y dark re - treat,
Christ on ___ earth with us doth dwell,

Beth - le - hem seek this ho - ly night.
And all our sweet - est mu - sic bring."
"Re, mi, fa, sol," in ac - cents sweet.
Join in the shout, "No - el, No - el!"

From *The International Book of Christmas Carols* by Walter Ehret and George K. Evans. Copyright © 1963 by Walter Ehret and George K. Evans. Reprinted by permission of the publisher, Viking Penguin, a division of Penguin Books USA, Inc.

Carol of the Birds

Traditional Catalonian

Traditional Catalonian Carol

1. Up - on this ho - ly night, When God's great star ap -
2. The Night - in - gale is first To bring his song of
3. The an - sw'ring Spar - row cries: "God comes to earth this
4. The Par - tridge adds his note: "To Beth - le - hem I'll

pears, And floods the earth with bright ~ ness,
cheer, And tell us of his glad ~ ness:
day A - mid the an - gels fly ~ ing."
fly, Where in the stall he's ly ~ ing.

Birds' voic - es rise in song, And, warb - ling all night
"Je - sus, our Lord, is born To free us from all
Trill - ing in sweet - est tones, The finch his Lord now
There, near the man - ger blest, I'll build my - self a

Dear Nightingale, Awake

Franconian Folk Carol

Bamberger Gesangbuch, 1670

1. Dear Night-in-gale, a - wake! And from the boughs of ev -'ry tree, Come
2. To his poor bed now fly, My lit -tle sis-ter, with your song, A-
3. Sing on and on and on; A hun-dred times a thou-sand ways Seek

trill the news most joy -ful - ly, A - wake, dear bird, a - wake! Our
muse the ba - by all day long, Oh, do not let him cry! In
there the pre-cious babe to praise, Till all his fears are gone. Our

Lord is born! Here from heav-en is sal - va-tion to us giv-en,
fin -est tones Mu - sic bring-ing, an-thems sing-ing, car-ols ring-ing,
Sav-ior's here! Hon- or show-ing, rap-ture glow-ing, love o'er-flow-ing,

Sing, sing,_ sing_ To hail_ the _ new - born King.
Sing, sing,_ sing_ To please_ the _ new - born King.
Sing, sing,_ sing_ To praise_ the _ new - born King.

From *The International Book of Christmas Carols* by Walter Ehret and George K. Evans. Copyright © 1963 by Walter Ehret and George K. Evans. Reprinted by permission of the publisher, Viking Penguin, a division of Penguin Books USA, Inc.

Chanticleer

W. Austin

Traditional English
arr. Martin Shaw

King Herod and the Cock

Traditional English Traditional English Carol

1. There was a star in David's land, So bright it did appear Into King Herod's chamber, And brightly it shined there.
2. The wise men soon espied it, And told the king on high, A princely babe was born that night No king could e'er destroy.
3. "If this be true," King Herod said, "As thou hast told to me, This roasted cock that lies in the dish Shall crow full fences three."
4. The cock soon thrustened and feathered well, By the work of God's own hand, And he did crow full fences three, In the dish where he did stand.

From *The Oxford Book of Carols*. Reprinted by permission of Oxford University Press, Oxford.

The Birds

Czech Carol
tr. O.B.C.

Czech Carol

1. From out of a wood did a cuc-koo fly, Cuc-koo, He
2. A pi-geon flew o-ver to Gal – i – lee, Vrer-croo, He
3. A dove set-tled down up-on Naz – a – reth, Tsu-croo, And

came to a man-ger with joy-ful cry, Cuc-koo; He
strut-ted and cooed and was full of glee, Vrer-croo; And
ten-der-ly chant-ed with all his breath: Tsu-croo; "O

hopped, he curt-sied, round he flew, And loud his
showed with jew-elled wings un-furled, His joy that
you," he cooed, "so good and true, My beau-ty

ju – bi – la-tion grew, Cuc-koo, cuc-koo, cuc-koo.
Christ was in the world, Vrer-croo, vrer-croo, vrer-croo.
do I give to you—Tsu-croo, tsu-croo, tsu-croo."

Christmas Close to Euphrates

ELIZABETH
CARAMAN
PAYNE

I was born and lived the first 16 years of my life in the central part of Turkey, in the village of Habousie on the banks of the ancient Euphrates River. The Euphrates is one of the four rivers that surrounded the Garden of Eden and is the only one that kept its original name. According to local tradition, Adam's Cave across the river to the west of Habousie was the place where Adam and Eve came to live after they were driven out of the Garden of Eden. Mount Ararat towers high above in the mountain range some 200 miles to the west, its snow-capped top a beacon to travelers coming from the east into the river valley where our village was located. Ours was a Christian village with a population of about 1000.

Armenia was one of the great nations of ancient times. It occupied what is now modern Turkey, part of Greece, Syria, and some of Iran. In A.D. 303 the Armenian king made Christianity the state religion, and from then on Armenia became a target for nations around it, first by the Persians, then much later by the Moslems. In 1453 the Turks captured Constantinople, the capital of the Eastern Roman empire. Armenia became a subject nation and the victim of periodic massacres at the hands of the Turks.

Most Armenians were members of the Eastern Orthodox church until about 1820 when Catholic missionaries from France and Protestant missionaries from America, Denmark, Germany, and Sweden came to Turkey. Unsuccessful in their attempts to convert the Turks, they turned to the Armenians and introduced many changes, such as replacing the classical Armenian Bible (which the Gregorian church used) with the modern Armenian Bible. In addition they opened schools, orphanages, and hospitals. The Protestant church in our community was founded by my father in about 1906 with the help of American missionaries whom he had come to know while attending their school in Brussa, a suburb of Constantinople. Still we regarded the Eastern Orthodox church or the Gregorian church as "the mother church."

I came to America in 1920 at the age of 16. Yet at Christmastime I always return in memory to my village of Habousie and the year 1913 when my family was still together.

CHRISTMAS PREPARATIONS

Our preparations for Christmas actually began about the first week of July when the luscious black and white, seedless mulberries—"as big as a woman's thumb"—and juicy apricots ripened. Authoritative sources indicate that apricots were first grown in Armenia and, according to tradition, the apricot was the first fruit Adam and Eve ate. Everyone agreed with the Bible that the tree was "pleasant to the sight and good for food." We children found it an easy tree to climb and pleasant to sit in beneath its thick leaves while we ate our fill of its fruit.

No one picked or ate any fruit, however, until baskets of ripe firstfruits were taken to the mother church and blessed by the priest. The fruit was then distributed to all who were present. I always tried to attend that service in order to get some of that blessed fruit to bring home and eat with my family. After the distribution of fruit, the "Thank you, God" song was sung and the choir chanted a well-known Gregorian chant. We then reverently and silently departed.

From that evening on we picked all fruits as they ripened, making them into preserves or drying them in the sun. Grapes did not ripen before the end of August, at which time we had a special day of blessing, for only then might they be picked and eaten. Anyone who was found eating fruit before it was blessed was avoided until he or she admitted his or her disobedience publicly in church, at which time the priest touched the penitent on the head, making the person one of us again.

> **I**n midsummer the first goodies from fruits and fruit juices were made, then put at once into crocks, which were sealed until the Christmas dinner.

In midsummer the first goodies from fruits and fruit juices were made, then put at once into crocks, which were sealed until the Christmas dinner. Before they were sealed away, however, we children between the ages of five and 10 were called upon to watch over the sweets, which were spread on linen cloth laid on the flat roofs. Our task was to keep the birds from picking at them. We stood like sentries, holding long brooms made from mulberry branches, watchful lest the birds spoil the goodies! Luckily for all of us, the hot sun dried our sweets in one day.

December was largely devoted to preparation for Christmas. Special pastries were made and put aside for Christmas Day dinner. All members of the family had to have baths before Christmas. Women and girls over 10 years old washed their hair and had it braided into as many as 30 braids. These braids would last through the winter until the first Saturday after Good Friday.

In preparation for winter, long, narrow wool scarves were made for the old people to wrap around their midriffs to keep their kidneys warm, stemming from the belief that most physical ailments of the elderly in winter were caused from cold in the kidneys. Among children, it was from cold, wet feet. So it was seen to that everyone who went to church on Christmas Eve and Christmas morning was dressed warmly.

THE PROTESTANT CELEBRATION

Beginning with the First Sunday in Advent, our Protestant church held services every evening, except Saturday. After the services we all went to the neighborhood stable room, one owned by a large family. Each street had one such large room with a large fireplace in which burned dried bricks made of dung mixed with fine straw. There each of us, young and old alike, was given a basket of cotton pods, from which we pulled cotton and listened as Aram Amou, our local storyteller, entertained us with traditional stories, legends, and water carrier's tales, as well as his own creations. One of his water carrier tales, of the holy family in flight, I shall never forget:

"En route to Egypt the holy family entered a cave to rest. That night a spider spun a web across the opening of the cave so the baby Jesus would not catch cold. Then Herod's soldiers came searching, looking everywhere for the newborn king. One sol-

> *Christmas Eve procession started about eleven o'clock…. Each person lighted a yellow wax candle, which no wind could blow out. Holding that in one hand and a gift for baby Jesus in the other, we made our way down the snow-lined street.*

dier turned to enter the cave but his companion deterred him, saying, 'Don't you see that spiderweb? It has taken days to make. We are looking for a babe who was taken away yesterday. Come, come, no one has gone into that cave for months.' And so again God kept the holy family safe."

It took Aram Amou an hour to tell that story. In the tradition of Near Eastern storytellers he used every part of his body when speaking. He raised his eyebrows, tilted his head, shrugged his shoulders, paused to heighten the dramatic moment. We youngsters, caught up in the drama, sighed and cried, "Don't let them get in!"

The evening before Christmas we finished picking the cotton balls at the stable room. This evening was called "Forgiveness Time." Aram Amou again told a story, this time about Christ, who told his followers to forgive and who himself forgave those who crucified him. Then Aram Amou encouraged anyone who harbored some resentment against another to stand and confess their lack of forgiveness and to be reconciled. My heart literally jumped in my chest when I saw three women and one man stand up and admit their sin. Then they embraced each other. Finally, Arom Amou lifted his aged arms high and prayed, "Almighty God, we all rejoice that all our people will be in church Christmas morning to welcome the baby Jesus who will deliver us from our sins." Then everyone embraced the four who had confessed. Tears of joy ran down every cheek.

We always had a Christmas program on December 25 at our Protestant church, but we all considered the real Christmas and the New Year to fall on January 6. On that day, we all joined in as the Gregorian, or mother church, celebrated that festive, holy day.

CHRISTMAS EVE

On January 5, the day before the Orthodox Christmas, every home was busier than a beehive in May and June—not because there was last-minute shopping or Christmas card writing or gift wrapping to do, but because of last-minute sewing of clothing to be worn that evening that had to be done. Also special food had to be prepared for the pilgrims who would come from three

nearby villages, where Christians were few among Moslem dwellers. Two rooms equipped with fireplaces were built especially for Orthodox pilgrims at the Gregorian church. These hardy pilgrims trudged through deep snow, carrying little children on their backs, and arrived just before dark. Our villagers provided for all their needs, including food, bedding, and even new mittens and sweaters for the children.

Children under seven were bathed and dressed in clean clothing, then sent to the community stable room and kept busy with games and stories. Grand-fathers saw to it that the children did not enter the stable itself and get dirty.

Others busily prepared the yellow wax candles that had been made weeks before and rolled into large balls. Now they were cut in half-yard long pieces and folded over to fit into the hand. These were to be held lighted while going to the mother church on Christmas Eve. In the late afternoon, four people from each street took white candles to the mother church and placed them throughout the building.

Men and teenage boys kept busy widening the path through the snow going

down the middle of the street. Sometimes the snow packed against our mud-brick walls reached as high as the roofs. Our houses were connected wall-to-wall with each other, and all seven streets led to the large, white, domed mother church in the center of the village. This had been built by the people themselves out of stone, some of it marble, that had

been carried piece by piece from as far away as a day's journey. (We did not measure distance by miles, but by days or half-day journeys a person could make walking.) The mother church stood high above our little village in the center of town. When I was little I thought the reason God could see us all was because he lived above the dome of the mother church.

Before we set out for the mother church we dressed. We also brought out our bedding from its rolled-up position in the closet and laid it out for the night. Under my pillow I found a new pair of gloves—up to then I had

only mittens—along with long, red wool stockings. My sister Acabie found colorful mittens and a knitted cap. Father found a beautiful red waist shawl that was to be wrapped around his middle. He said, "That will surely keep more than just my kidneys warm." My mother had knitted them all, yet we had never seen her doing it. She must have done it all after we had gone to bed.

CANDLELIT PROCESSION

Christmas Eve procession started about eleven o'clock (though we had neither clocks nor watches). Each person lighted a yellow wax candle, which no wind could blow out. Holding that in one hand and a gift for baby Jesus in the other, we made our way down the snow-lined street.

I shall never forget that 1913 Christmas Eve procession. My mother had told me I would be one of "God's helpers" that night. Also it was the first time my little sister had gone with us. Previously my Aunt Zedug had come and stayed with her. That procession was special, too, because it was not snowing, and the stars had never seemed so bright. In the starlit night I could see the high white dome of the mother church almost touching the sky. Lastly, the sight of the procession was memorable, with each person holding a yellow wax candle along the length of the dark street. Surely, I imagined, God was seated in that beautiful dome, clapping his hands with joy in approval of our procession.

We approached the Byzantine arched doorway and walked through it into

the foyer. There we left our shoes, for no one ever entered the church (or a home, for that matter) with shoes on. We also put down our yellow candles, for we would need them on the way home, and left our family gifts for the "friends of baby Jesus" in the gift room. My father had carried a heavy bag of cracked wheat, my mother a large bowl of yogurt. I carried a bag of figs and dates. All gifts had to be of the best. They were intended for the pilgrims who had come from nearby villages. Besides food, there were gifts of warm clothing, as well as grain and flour.

The dimly lit church brightened as more candles were lighted. Pots of charcoal fire were placed at each window. Soft chants sounded as if they came from an angel chorus. Burning incense filled the air as the priest swung his censer while walking around. The church bells began ringing loudly again and at the same moment the curtains were pulled aside to reveal a painting of the nativity illuminated by a candle as large as a man. The Holy Spirit, depicted as a dove, hovered above the baby Jesus lying on the straw. Mary, on her knees, adored the child while Joseph stood to one side with folded hands, looking down upon the Promised One, an awed expression on his face.

At this time my mother took hold of my hand and said, "Come, we must go now." We older children and adults were taken as a group to the pilgrims' rooms where we were given our assignments. Before Christmas each house that was thought to be in need had been visited by the priest or by church officers and responsible Christians, including my mother and father. We did not have poor districts in our village. Living wall to wall we knew who was poor and who was not. For instance, next to us lived a widow and her daughter-in-law. They needed whatever we could leave at their house—candles, matches, thread, yarn, salt, and other foodstuffs. My mother had taken me along on her fact-finding visits. My duty was to read the Scriptures to the folks while my mother discreetly lifted the lids of the flour barrel, the bulgur crock, and the pickle barrel. Then on Christmas Eve it became our duty to deliver needed gifts to these households while the worshipers were away at the service.

We all returned to the church in time to see the pageant of the priest and altar boys in their gorgeous robes, followed by the choir, going through the worshipers as they chanted heavenly music. For me the swinging censer had a very special Christmas thrill that sent shivers of inward happiness flooding through me. I felt like I was rubbing elbows with God. The choir chanted, "A happy new year and a happy Christ's birthday." The carved figures of the apostles around us seemed to come alive, each one breathing a life of its own. All of the while the voices of the choirboys sounded an ancient Gregorian chant that filled the church.

As we returned to our homes, our yellow candles almost burned away, I remarked, "I can see why poor people believe that God and the angels have come and filled those crocks. Only with their help could we humans have done all that in such a short time."

To this my mother said, "Jesus taught us how we Christians must provide for the needs of others since we are all the children of one Father." In those simple words she helped me to see my role as a child of God in relation to my neighbor.

Home at last, we fell asleep at once and woke only when Mother shook us. We had to get dressed for the Christmas Day service in the Gregorian church.

CHRISTMAS DAY

Christmas Day was one of a glorious sun reflected everywhere in the snow. The ancient Euphrates River was frozen from shore to shore that morning, and it became the pathway over which pilgrims walked in single file to the church. The church had no special flowers or decorations. But the white, red, and green lighted candles lent a special glow to the sanctuary, into which sunlight flowed from the dome above. There were no seats, so worshipers stood patiently through the service.

After the service everyone greeted each other, saying, "Happy New Year and Merry Christmas!" They then embraced and kissed each other on the cheek. Young women and girls kissed the back of the hands of older men.

Next, we younger ones walked to the village spring. There, people suffering with malaria climbed the mulberry tree on the banks of the spring and shook the icicles that hung from its branches, crying out, "Who wants mulberries?"

We shouted back from below, "What? Mulberries at this season? That can't be!"

The climbers shouted back, "Then there should be no malaria chills."

To this we replied, "No, there won't be any after this Christmas morning."

Then we all bowed our heads and prayed, "Dear God, take away Dikrna's (or Mariam's, etc.) malaria." Many of our climbers declared afterwards that they never again had the malaria chills.

> *From time to time, messages came from other houses where feasts were in progress. They told us of the mysterious filling of crocks by unseen hands and of choice gifts.*

THE COMMUNITY DINNER

Finally, a special horn blower on each street was directed to sound the signal for our Christmas dinner. At each community gathering place 15 or more low tables had been set up. We children were seated at one end, with the young women and men in the middle and the older people at the head. Everyone in the entire village had the same menu.

The dinner lasted a long time, for many of the older folk told stories of Christians who through the centuries had given their lives that we now could enjoy the privilege of Christmas. Also, from time to time, messages came from other houses where feasts were in progress. They told us of the mysterious filling of crocks by unseen hands and of choice gifts: "Degin Arshalou's crocks were filled when she came home from church! She wants you all to praise the Lord for his thoughtfulness."

At last the time came for consuming the crocks of sweets that had been filled and sealed during the season of ripening fruits. Only grandmothers were allowed to open the crocks; the sweets were then distributed by the eldest sons' wives.

Rojij and *basdagh*, very special sweets made from fruit juices and nuts, were associated with Christmas and no other season of the year. Dates, figs, and small oranges were brought out and given to all. They had been brought to us on camels from Arabia and Palestine in exchange for our wheat, barley, and cotton the previous October. The small oranges were saved for grandmothers, who used their fragrant peels for their herb snuff.

Near the end of this cooperative Christmas meal, we girls were given one special gift by the new bride. Boys received one from the groom. Both gifts were some kind of toy.

Finally, at the end of the meal a short prayer of thanks was made by the oldest grandfather present. Then we all stood and chanted the Lord's Prayer in classical Armenian. This was the one time I felt for sure Christ was in our midst, teaching us a new precious pattern for prayer. At

its conclusion an awesome silence filled us all with reverence and gratitude.

There was still time for each family to go to its own house before the evening service. Everyone was anxious to see what God had left for them or what crock had been filled. My sister and I usually made a wild dash for home so that we might search carefully before our parents got there. "Here is a basket of newly baked bread with gobs of sesame seeds on the top!" my sister exclaimed.

"Here is an embroidered cover for Mother's Bible!" I cried.

Mother chimed in, "See how our pickle crock is full again." As we smelled the appetizing odor of garlic and dill I saw my mother's eyes moisten, and I remembered how in August, when my younger aunt from the city was visiting us, she had rebuked Mother for giving away our cucumbers.

"Why don't you fill up your own pickle crock first?" she asked.

My mother had looked at her and replied, "Because we want our crock to be filled with thoughtfulness and love at Christmastime."

It was then that I began to see why my rich and clever mother, who could have learned how to make bread, had chosen to remain ignorant and to be in need of things that others could give us. What others gave us, she would say, God had a hand in.

While we were rejoicing we heard the familiar tap, tap sound on our wall. I ran to the wall closet, opened the door, pulled out the loose brick, and came face-to-face with our excited neighbor, whose wall adjoined ours.

"Just think," she exclaimed, "God has given us a whole roll of material for head cover-

> There were no thank-you notes to be written, for all had given their best to others in the name of God and for God's glory.

ings! Oh, and Degen Bayzar has sent word to tell your mother that they have enough printed material to make Azniv's dress. All of you praise God for his thoughtfulness."

Then I told her what God had left for us and how happy we all were to be remembered by him. "God never forgets anybody," were her final words as she put her own brick back in place.

Turning to my family I asked, "Mother, didn't you buy all those things at uncle's store last summer?

"Not I," she replied, "but God, who helps us to think of everyone's needs."

And so for us Christmas was a holy time because it began that way. The holiday celebrations came the day after. "Not I, but God" was the spirit of Christmas. There were no thank-you notes to be written, for all had given their best to others in the name of God and for God's glory. ❖

Whistles from the Past

With lights blazing, the Lionel No. 408 locomotive arrives at the station. This standard gauge set in apple green sold for $82.50 when first introduced in 1927. Courtesy of M. Levitt, Minneapolis.

BY PETER KIZILOS

Down through the ages, toys, especially miniatures, have fascinated and delighted young and old alike. Some of the small clay boats and chariots unearthed by archaeologists in distant lands date from 5000 years ago. The ancient Egyptian, Cretan, and Sumerian civilizations provide evidence that crafting scaled-down versions of everyday objects is a well-established human tradition.

Miniatures—from dolls and houses to cars, boats, planes, and even spaceships—continue to make excellent gifts in modern times. One of the most popular miniatures, a staple of the Christmas shopping list, is the model train. From the most primitive early toys to the sleekest,

most sophisticated railroad sets of today, models of the "iron horse" have a way of sparking our imagination, of bringing the sights and sounds of mysterious and exotic places to life. Letting the imagination roam, you may find yourself settling into a comfortable berth on the Orient Express or Trans-Siberia Railroad, feeling the rhythmic pitching of the train, and watching the world go by. In a day and age of airplane travel, when we all seem in a hurry to get somewhere, trains recall a time when the journey itself was an adventure.

Many people who were introduced to trains as young children have never lost their fascination with them. As a result, many adults continue to enjoy the hobby of model train collecting. In fact, the Train Collectors Association, a group of toy

train collectors, is the largest organized toy group in the world. These collectors recapture the magic of childhood fantasy by collecting the toy trains of yesteryear and modeling the long-vanished routes of famous trains from the past.

Though both model and toy trains conjure up images of adventure and romance, train lovers and collectors make an important distinction between the two. The toys, which were manufactured first, are fanciful creations intended to stir the imagination. Models, on the other hand, are built to satisfy an engineer's eye for detail. *Scale* models are *exact* reproductions of the "giant beasts" themselves.

It's easy to see why the early toy trains strike such a receptive chord. These visually stunning creations are painted in many different colors and emblazoned with beautiful lithographic designs. The shiny orange boxcars, brown and yellow topped passenger cars, green and silver freight cars, and, of course, black locomotives with red or silver painted trim are beautiful, decorative pieces. Add scenery, railroad stations, storefronts, landscaped gardens, and people, and you start to appreciate the beauty and wonder of train collection!

Just as there are many different types of trains, train collectors come in all types. Some people specialize in collecting toy trains, others in the models. Some collectors seek to amass a complete set of trains produced by a given manufacturer, such as Lionel.

Train collecting can be a serious hobby, demanding some engineering expertise in addition to an appreciation of antiques.

People with a special interest in toy trains, as opposed to models, especially enjoy hunting for new items to add to their collection. While the toy trains may not run very well, if at all, they do make

impressive display items. Many of the trains prized by toy collectors were originally given as Christmas gifts. Children often played with these trains for a while, then lost interest, so they were stored away on a shelf somewhere. Often they remain in excellent condition.

Model train collectors, on the other hand, are generally more interested in getting their trains up and running. They usually have a layout down in the basement and keep their trains well-maintained. The more artistic model train enthusiasts enjoy fashioning the scenery surrounding the train, making the trees, bushes, and train stations, buildings, and other visual elements around and about the track. These model train buffs recreate a world when trains were king of the transportation system.

The research needed to reproduce the details of a historic railroad line faithfully is often extensive. This is one of the more absorbing aspects of the hobby for some scale model train enthusiasts. To model a particular train, for example, it might be

necessary to dig up old train schedules or comb through history books to see how many cars and of what types these trains had and with what kind of equipment they were loaded.

Other hobbyists are more intrigued by the nuts and bolts of model trains. They spend less time fussing over the artistic layout of the track itself and the surrounding scenery, preferring tinkering needed to keep their trains in good mechanical condition. Given the complexity of some model engines, those with an interest in engineering find plenty of work to keep them busy.

HISTORY OF TRAINS

Though steam trains and locomotives were not invented until the nineteenth century, the fundamental idea of trains goes back much further in time. The ancient Romans developed a paved railway system for beast-drawn wagons. Horse-drawn wagons—popular in the coal-mining regions of England—were built on the same basic idea and transported

Two trains by American Flyer arrive and depart via Lionel's unique models of the Hellgate bridge over New York's East River. The wide-gauge observation car of the 1928 Hamiltonian set in Victory Red strikes a Christmasy note. The Grand Canyon wide-gauge freight set No. 1496 included a magnificent steam locomotive (shown), sand car, hopper car, tank car, machinery car, stock car, and caboose. Courtesy of M. Levitt, Minneapolis.

These "O" scale models of the 1930 Great Northern Railways locomotive, built by Samhongsa of Korea, are shown to contrast the brass finish done by the factory with a custom finish painted in Glacier Park colors. Courtesy of W. Praus, Minneapolis.

coal from the mines to river loading sites. Both are close cousins to the modern trains of today.

Trains became a prominent fixture in the middle and latter part of the nineteenth century, dramatically altering the landscape of the United States. They opened up whole new areas for development and bridged vast territorial expanses, making it possible for the United States to survive as a large nation. Towns sprang up along the railways and people migrated to areas served by trains. No longer did pioneers have to make the far more risky horse and wagon trek from East to West. Instead, railroad passengers could ride in relative comfort and safety from one end of the nation to the other.

The railroad also played an important role during the Civil War, giving the Union army the advantage of greater mobility. In recognition of their importance, many trains were decorated with patriotic symbols.

Soon, people everywhere were eager to own a part of this exciting transportation revolution, to experience a bit of the magic and optimism symbolized by the opening of vast new vistas for exploration and travel. It didn't take long for toymakers to see the potential market for models based on the new "iron horse." Miniature versions of the giant trains appeared almost simultaneously with the creation of the real thing.

TOY TRAINS

Some of the very first miniature trains were made by German crafters in the 1830s. These mechanical toys could be pushed along a track, but had no independent means of propulsion. These early toy trains were made by pouring molten metal, usually brass or tin, into a mold, the same way other popular toys of the era—including tin soldiers—were fashioned. Hand-carved wooden fittings were then fastened to these metal bases to create a complete toy train. Although these models were often quite attractive, they were fragile and usually had no moving parts.

The French, who were master tinsmiths, produced charming and elaborately crafted toy trains. Many of these had no rails and were pushed along the floor. Their ornate designs, tall chimneys, and spidery spoked wheels were quite fanciful and attractive. Because paint does not adhere well to tin, these early French models are rarely found with their paintwork intact.

In Britain, the birthplace of the Industrial Revolution, toymakers took model train manufacturing seriously enough. Sir Henry Wood, a music conductor and early toy train devotee, is credited with being one of the first inventors to build a steam-powered toy. "Dribblers" and "piddlers" (steam-powered trains nick-named for the tell-tale trail of water deposited by their steam cylinders) were among the first British-made products.

Many of the early toy train makers were also instrument makers. Because the early steam-powered trains made such a mess, toymakers started fitting the trains with clockwork mechanisms—a more effective and safe means of locomotion. Firms such as Newton & Co. of London produced highly complex and elegant brass models for the children of wealthy families. There was little attempt to make these trains realistic or scale models. Rather, they were designed to capture the imagination. These engineering marvels now make beautiful display pieces in transportation museums.

The handcrafted toy trains made in Europe could not be profitably produced and sold in the United States. To sell at competitive prices, trainmakers had to be able to mass produce the trains.

Toymakers in the United States were quick to start building toy trains of their own. Mathias Baldwin, founder of the Baltimore Locomotive Works, fashioned an early passenger train model—a locomotive and several cars—in the 1830s. By the late 1830s, several of the great American toymakers had toy trains rolling out their doors. George W. Brown & Co., of Forestville, Connecticut, produced the first known self-propelled American model train (a clockwork version) in 1856.

American-made trains were different from the European versions. To be successful in the American market, manufacturers had to be ready to ship toy trains vast distances. Under these conditions, American toy trains had to be more rugged and durable than their more delicate French counterparts, and more sophisticated than the German lead and wood trains or the British "dribblers."

The typical American toy train design was made of heavy tinplate. The locomotive was the standard toy item; cars and track were virtually nonexistent in America during the early days.

Between 1860 and 1890—the golden age of American tin train making—the big toy train makers were Ives; Althof Bergman & Co.; Hull & Stafford; Francis, Field & Francis; and James Fallows. From the 1890s to just before World War I, many of these same companies produced much more realistic trains at reasonable prices. In a few short decades, most middle-class families found model trains within their reach.

MODEL TRAINS

As public interest in model trains grew, people began to demand more sophistication and realism. Toymakers responded by producing more elaborate toys, with more details and better working parts. The era of the model train, as opposed to the toy train, was ushered in during this period. Models, as opposed to toys, were far more complex

mechanically. They were also much more exact replicas of actual trains.

During the second era of miniature train manufacturing, from about 1890 to 1900, toy trains zoomed off in a new direction. Before then, manufacturers had mostly thought of trains as stand-alone items; like toy boats they were complete unto themselves. In the 1890s, train makers introduced full-blown toy train sys-

Toy trains by a variety of manufacturers are pictured here. All are "O" gauge sets, but range in original price from $1.50 to $97.50. From bottom to top: Lionel-Ives clockwork set from 1933; Mickey Mouse Circus Train by Lionel from 1935; Louis Marx Co. Streamliner M-10005; Lionel's streamlined torpedo locomotive No. 1688E with pullman cars and observation car; Lionel Work Train No. 277W from 1837; Hiawatha passenger train set by American Flyer, No. 1741, from 1936; the 1990 version of the "Rail Chief" from 1937 by Lionel. Courtesy of M. Levitt and W. Praus, Minneapolis.

tems, with tracks, passenger cars, wagons, stations, and the works. Electric trains soon followed.

Theodore Marklin of Germany was one of the first and most successful toy train makers in Europe. In 1891, his company came out with the first sectional track and, a year later, created a sensation by introducing a figure-eight layout. Marklin also produced the first electric train sets sold in Europe in 1898.

The Bing brothers, also from Germany, did much to popularize model trains in the public mind. Bing's model railroad display at the

Paris Exhibition of 1900, a miniature Midland Railway engine, attracted a lot of attention. During the Paris show, Stefan Bing agreed to produce a more realistic model train in cooperation with W. J. Bassett-Lowke, a British firm. Together, Bing and Bassett-Lowke helped transform the concept of playing with trains into a popular recreation. In later years, Bing encouraged interest in model trains as a hobby by distributing a publication titled *The Little Railway Engineer*, a guidebook for assembling model railroad layouts.

As the demand for trains exploded over the years, manufacturers sought more inexpensive methods to make trains. While the toys were produced relatively inexpensively, the more sophisticated models remained quite expensive to produce. As train-making technology improved, along with marketing practices, the price gradually came down. In the pre-World War I era, these toys became more affordable and more widely available. The consumer market was catching on.

It was in this era that some of the more famous names in American train making started to compete for customers. Ives, Lionel, and American Flyer produced some of the most popular trains during this period. The Ives company, established by Edward R. Ives in 1868, became famous for its slogan "Ives toys make happy boys." The company was known for the quality of its products and its excellent replacement service. Two of the more dramatic Ives products were a cast-iron engine that plumed smoke from a lighted cigarette and another that fired caps.

Lionel, a legendary name in American train making, remains practically synonymous with model trains. Established by Joshua Lionel Cohen in the early 1900s, Lionel produced, and still produces, the best-known line of American model trains. Cohen began his venture into toy train making by manufacturing small electric motors. He decided to use these motors to power electric trains. After World War I, Lionel became the biggest name in model train making, eclipsing other European and American manufacturers.

Lionel succeeded so well because its trains were more realistic than its competitors, had powerful motors, and were ruggedly constructed. By the 1920s, Lionel trains had become the standard of excellence for judging toy train manufacturers in America. During this period, the firm also introduced more brightly colored trains—in brilliant blues, light greens, rich tans, primary reds, and other innovative colors. The new look created a sensation and contributed to Lionel's growing success.

American Flyer, another famous name in the model train business, sought to compete directly with Lionel by producing larger and cheaper trains. It enjoyed some success in the 1920s with an expanded line of larger, ornately decorated passenger trains. Lionel, however, responded by producing an even more impressive and elaborate line of models and eventually took over American Flyer in 1967.

Model train manufacturers gradually began to eclipse the toy train industry, which had reached its greatest popularity and most highly developed state before World War I. Post-World War II trains are much more detailed than the pre-war variety and are the most popular among those who actually run model trains.

Train collectors of all types often attend conventions to meet other model train lovers, exchange notes, and talk about trains. Twice a year, the Train Collectors Association sponsors a train collectors meeting in York, Pennsylvania. It's not unusual for up to 4000 collectors to attend. On the local level, train clubs often sponsor meetings and set up layouts where the public can be enchanted by model trains in action.

Collectors and modelers alike often bring their families to gatherings of train hobbyists. These events can be good places to rekindle a love for trains. Some people need only a gentle nudge to relive a special Christmas morning when they unwrapped that shiny new American Flyer or Lionel train of their dreams. Memories of childhood and the magic of model and toy trains are often inseparable. ❖

A Christmas sight to delight any child, this peacock blue "O" gauge train set by Lionel sold for $14.00 in 1929. Courtesy of W. Praus, Minneapolis.

A Christmas Alphabet

MARGARET BURCH-JONES

A is for the Angel that sang a joyful song.

B is for the Baby who laughed out loud and strong.

C is for the Camel that worked on Christmas Day.

D is for the Donkey that munched upon the hay.

E is for the Earthen jar that held the baby's milk.

F is for the Friendly Fox with eyes as soft as silk.

G is for the Gentle Goat that bleated long and low.

H is for the Huntsman who threw away his bow.

I is for the Incense—
a gift the Magi
brought.

J is for the Jesus
babe whom the
Magi sought.

K is for the Kitten
that warmed his
little toes.

L is for the Loving
Lamb that nuzzled
with its nose.

M is for the Mother
of the swaddled
baby dear.

N is for the
Nightingale that
whispered in her ear.

O is for the Oxen
that round the
manger came.

P is for the Peasant
boy who called the
King by name.

Q is for the Quail that
helped the shepherd
watch his flock.

R is for the Robin
that sat upon a rock.

S is for the Shining
Star that lit their path
that night.

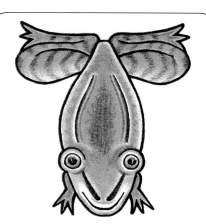

T is for the Tiny
Toad that sang with
all his might.

U is for the Unicorn
that loitered by the stall.

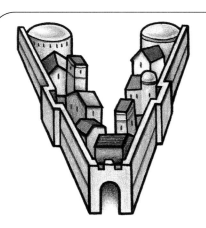

V is for the Village
that slumbered through
it all.

W is for the Watchful
Wren that whispered in
the loft.

X is for the eXtra
straw that made the
cradle soft.

Y is for the Yarn
that spun a blanket
for his chest.

Z is for the Zither
that lulled the babe
to rest.

Our Christmas

~

Christmas Eve

_____
_____
_____
_____
_____

Christmas Day

_____
_____
_____
_____
_____

Christmas Worship

_____
_____
_____

Christmas Guests   ## Christmas Gifts

_____   _____
_____   _____
_____   _____
_____   _____
_____   _____